C000006119

*"Caroline Cox is remarkabl[...]
controversial; always comp[...]
records her profound servic[...]
marginalised people."*

Rt Revd Philip Mounstephen, Bishop of Truro

*"I have long admired Baroness Cox and have travelled with
her into notorious international danger zones.* Eyewitness to
a Broken World *is an inspiring account of her tireless work
on behalf of persecuted Christians in some of the world's most
troubled countries."*

Frank Wolf, Former U.S. Congressman

*"In a lifetime of dedicated service in many countries, Baroness Cox
has been a courageous voice of the voiceless in what she describes
as a 'broken world'. Her book reminds us of the thin veneer of
civilisation under which we live. It is both fascinating and
revealing reading."*

Lord Singh of Wimbledon

*"In a world darkened by conflict and human rights abuses,
Baroness Caroline Cox stands as a beacon of light. Her tireless
efforts for the persecuted and marginalised, regardless of their
faith or background, are exemplary."*

**Raheel Raza, President, Council for Muslims
Facing Tomorrow**

*the world he saw around him. This had furnished,
to some of the world's most*

2ND EDITION

BARONESS
COX

Eyewitness to a broken world

LELA GILBERT

MONARCH
BOOKS

Text copyright © 2021 Lela Gilbert
This edition copyright © 2021 Lion Hudson IP Limited

The right of Lela Gilbert to be identified as the author of this work
has been asserted by her in accordance with the Copyright, Designs
and Patents Act 1988.

All rights reserved. No part of this publication may be reproduced
or transmitted in any form or by any means, electronic or mechanical, including
photocopy, recording, or any information storage and retrieval system, without
permission in writing from the publisher.

Published by **Monarch Books**
www.lionhudson.com
Part of the SPCK Group
SPCK, 36 Causton Street, London, SW1P 4ST

Paperback ISBN 978-1-8003-0017-0
eISBN 978-1-8003-0024-8

First edition 2007

Acknowledgments
Scripture quotations are taken from the Holy Bible, New International
Version, copyright © 1973, 1978, 1984 International Bible Society. Used by
permission of Hodder & Stoughton, a member of the Hodder Headline Group.
All rights reserved. 'NIV' is a trademark of International Bible Society. UK
trademark number 1448790.

Some quotes are taken from personal conversations between Caroline Cox and
those she spoke to.

Extracts pp. 42-44, 52-53 taken from Andrew Boyd, *Baroness Cox: A Voice for the
Voiceless* (Lion Hudson, 1998).

Extract p. 155 taken from 'Situation of human rights in the Sudan' by Gaspar
Biro, UN Secretary General, © 1995 United Nations. Reprinted with the
permission of the United Nations.

A catalogue record for this book is available from the British Library

Printed and bound in the United Kingdom, July 2021, LH26

Lela Gilbert is a writer and researcher who has authored or co-authored more than sixty published books. She writes primarily in the field of ecumenical Christian non-fiction, and her work includes the critically acclaimed *Saturday People, Sunday People: Israel through the Eyes of a Christian Sojourner* and *Persecuted: The Global Assault on Christians*, with Paul Marshall and Nina Shea. She has travelled extensively in Europe, Africa, Asia, and the Middle East as well as to many regions in North America. After a decade in Jerusalem, Israel, she now resides in the Washington DC area.

Contents

Foreword

Lord Alton of Liverpool

It was high time that a definitive account was written about the remarkable achievements of Caroline Cox. Lela Gilbert has gone about her task with great energy, doing justice to her subject. *Baroness Cox: Eyewitness to a Broken World* is well researched and well written. It is the perfect rebuttal of the defeatist view that because the world is a complex and inordinately brutal place, no individual can do anything much to change it.

Often we are intimidated by the scale of poverty, persecution, and violence. Headline figures – 2,000 dead in Darfur and 2 million displaced; many millions more racked by starvation or poverty, living below any rational definition of human decency; countless numbers caught in debt, bondage, trafficking, and slavery – these statistics can so easily intimidate us into inertia by their scale and the seemingly intractable problems they represent.

All too often we feel like the character in one of Robert Louis Stephenson's books, the young boy who plaintively cries, "The world is so big and I am so small, I do not like it at all, at all." Early on, Caroline Cox decided that she didn't much like it, either, but she decided to do something about it.

As Gilbert's account unfolds we see the genesis of an instinctive dislike of bullies, conditioned primarily by personal experiences in higher education – where Caroline Cox battled against Marxist intolerance.

These battles were the ideal preparation for her later travels in Eastern Europe, where the dead hand of Marxism had left a trail of oppression and destitution. During those early visits to Poland, Romania, and Russia she began to build the twin pillars of her work: advocacy for the underdog facing persecution and practical active compassion for the suffering victims.

Her experiences as a nurse and as a daughter of a distinguished surgeon would prove to be invaluable. In 1983, her elevation to the peerage on the recommendation of Margaret Thatcher subsequently provided the ideal forum in which to raise her voice for the voiceless.

Caroline often jokes that she was "a nurse by intention and a baroness by astonishment", but for us, her colleagues in the House of Lords, she is without equal in her bravery and dedication. The astonishment would be if there were not a place in Parliament for this rare breed.

In the years that followed her entry into Parliament she needed all her reserves of energy and all her formidable skills – especially during the next phase of her work in the 1990s in war-torn Armenia. In May 1991 she had been asked to lead a delegation of human rights experts from the Andrei Sakharov Memorial Congress in Moscow to assess the situation in Nagorno-Karabakh. Caroline Cox then mounted a systematic campaign to alert the West to the plight of that enclave and to ensure that adequate supplies and help reached its beleaguered people. It is little wonder that Armenia has honoured her bravery and consistency.

Her work in Armenia – of advocacy and relief – would create a template for the future and has taken her to Indonesia, Myanmar (also known as Burma), East Timor, Nigeria, Uganda, Syria, Sudan, and South Sudan. Its authenticity has been undergirded throughout by a willingness to expose herself to danger and a willingness to see things at first hand. What better evidence is there than that of an eyewitness?

On my own visits to Sudan and Darfur I have seen the scale of the attrition orchestrated by the former regime in Khartoum. With Caroline Cox I have travelled in North Korea. Without such first-hand encounters you can easily become anaesthetised to the scale of suffering and pain. Parliament also listens more attentively if it knows that you are not just reading out someone else's observations.

When I undertook an illegal visit across the border into the Karen state of Myanmar, the first group of tribal people I met asked me, "How is Lady Cox?" The question didn't surprise me. Caroline is not only respected for her bravery and knowledge, but genuinely loved by many who know that she has kept faith with them and ensured that the world has heard their story.

If you have ever wondered about the motivation behind the carnage in Sudan, or about the reasons why the Burmese military continue to murder their own people, Caroline Cox's first-hand encounters detailed in this book provide many of the answers. It isn't an academic dissertation, a dry-as-dust treatise, but an encounter with real people and real suffering, and it provides a clue as to what individuals can do to challenge the things they do not like. The fact that we can't solve *all* the problems of the world is no reason for not trying to solve *any* of them. This story also leads you to understand this woman's extraordinary faith, and how it drives her on.

Albert Einstein famously said that "the world is a dangerous place to live, not because of the people who are evil, but because of the people who don't do anything about it". After reading *Baroness Cox: Eyewitness to a Broken World*, you will surely agree that this is not an accusation that anyone will ever be able to level at Caroline Cox.

David Alton – Lord Alton of Liverpool – serves as an Independent cross-bench member of the House of Lords, was for eighteen years a Member of the House of Commons, and is Visiting Professor at Liverpool Hope University.

www.davidalton.net

Prologue

The Most Revd Dr Benjamin A. Kwashi

In the world today there are places that are hidden and unknown; communities that are broken, divided, suffering, and silent. Whether it is the result of political oppression, religious intolerance, war, famine, mankind's astonishing inhumanity, or other causes, darkness has invaded the lives of many and joy has fled. These are the people who have no means of making their voices heard – who can help them when no one even knows they exist?

It is into these situations that Baroness Caroline Cox has brought hope, light, and a reason for living. She has never hesitated to visit us in northern Nigeria – or any other church or country in the world – simply because there was danger or crisis. Indeed, she specialises in seeking out the hidden members of the persecuted church throughout the world, speaking for these who cannot make their voices heard and bringing their plight to the notice of the nations. She has used her position as a member of the House of Lords to the benefit of thousands of suffering Christians in many different countries. Others in the West offer to send aid to those who are persecuted – that aid may or may not arrive – but Baroness Cox comes herself.

Her eyewitness accounts, her photographs, her moving testimonies, and her deep personal compassion speak in ways that go beyond the actual words.

Twenty years ago, shortly before a major crisis erupted in northern Nigeria, we in the Christian church were feeling vulnerable, alone, and isolated. We knew that help was not going to come from the outside world and that trouble was brewing. Moreover, at that time we had relatively little information about the persecuted church in other countries – perhaps Christians in these places were feeling as we did, even though we did not know about them.

Then Caroline Cox came. She brought encouragement, hope, and the assurance that hundreds of people all around the world were praying. Her first biography opened our eyes to the plight of our brothers and sisters in so many different places. She was indeed a "voice for the voiceless" and a light in the darkness.

Since then she has made dozens more journeys to us, always bringing laughter and joy. Her journeys continue: she will never give up – she is made of sterner stuff. But wherever she goes, the deep, heartfelt gratitude of so many, many people follow her. Words cannot convey the admiration, the love, the thanks, and the sheer wonder of the persecuted church: how can anyone care so much?

Only the Lord can reward this remarkable lady, and surely he will do so.

Ben Kwashi is the Anglican Archbishop of Jos in Nigeria and General Secretary of GAFCON (Global Anglican Future Conference).

Chapter One

Appointment with the World

Baroness Cox of Queensbury – Caroline to her friends – is often described as a "voice for the voiceless", as one who works tirelessly on behalf of the world's most defenceless people. But this only begins to reflect the almost unbelievable contrasts in Caroline Cox's life – the juxtaposition of her elite status in the House of Lords and the rough-and-tumble world of her travels. She has, over two and a half decades, made innumerable journeys to dangerous and unforgiving locales on behalf of nearly forgotten peoples. She has seen with her own eyes the worst imaginable human suffering. She has wept, raged, and wrestled with her options. The conditions under which she travels are sometimes nearly intolerable; her accommodations far removed from the gilded glory of the Lords Chamber.

One of the most notorious of her destinations has been Sudan – a nation long torn asunder by war and repression, at times on a scale that can only be described as genocide. One particular episode in Sudan, prior to the South's independence in 2011, serves as a worthy introduction to Caroline Cox's *Eyewitness to a Broken World*.

Because her interests are in the people in the south of the country, before a ceasefire was in place she often travelled into southern Sudanese airspace illegally, flying into areas designated no-fly zones by the Khartoum government. The pilots who flew in and out of Southern Sudan risked their lives to do so, but they left their passengers on the ground with no firm schedule in place for a return flight. If the weather held, if there were no reports of government troops – only then did the pilots come back. And the flights were far from first class. Flying into South Sudan meant shivering for up to three hours in unpressurised, unheated cabins, being continually at risk from anti-aircraft weapons, and keeping a sharp eye out for fighter jets that bore the markings of various Arab nations – nations that had their own unreported reasons for patrolling the sky.

It was a risky business, but there was no alternative. The areas of Sudan that needed the closest scrutiny in respect of human rights could not be reached on commercial or relief flights. And the country is too large and the roads too impassable for much travel on the ground. So the unauthorised pilots filed a flight plan with air traffic controllers – but it was a plan that differed from the actual route to be taken. And at the end of the journey, death-defying landings bounced across short and narrow dirt airstrips that were sometimes transformed, in five minutes' time during the rainy season, into treacherous mud slicks.

Khartoum's no-fly zones were located precisely in those areas where the Sudanese government perpetrated its worst human rights atrocities. It was within these zones that religious persecution led to the slaughter of Muslims who refused to participate in jihad, or holy war, and of Christians who refused to convert to Islam. Here civilian men and boys were killed in cold blood and their surviving women and children captured and forced into slavery; here malnutrition and disease raged;

here such sordid atrocities as the mutilation of infants went unchallenged. For obvious reasons, the Khartoum regime forbade eyewitnesses from entering these areas, especially those with access to the international media.

Nonetheless, Caroline Cox continued to make the journey. Upon her arrival, she was greeted by throngs of joyful, singing Sudanese men, women, and children. Their faces alight with happiness, they quickly unloaded the plane and carried to their villages the supplies she had brought for them.

On one particular journey the heat on arrival in Bahr elEl-Ghazal was exceptionally intense, even for Sudan. As she stepped out of the plane, a blast of suffocating air pressed against her like a heavy weight. The temperature was well over 100 degrees Fahrenheit; dust and insects were everywhere. Travellers into those remote areas are warned about poisonous snakes, enormous camel spiders, scorpions, giant millipedes, and an assortment of other unfriendly creatures.

Baroness Cox is usually accompanied by two or three others when she visits Sudan, and it is their habit for each person to travel with a one-person tent. They sleep in proximity to the burnt-out ruins of a nearby village.

That night, after double-checking the tent floor for disturbing or dangerous intruders, she zipped herself safely inside. She was exhausted, longing for sleep, but the humidity seemed to be increasing with every passing moment. She finally managed to doze, but before long was awakened by a blaze of white light, followed almost immediately by enormous percussive blast. A thunderstorm rolled across the village, trailing behind it a cloudburst of unbelievable force.

The travellers' small tents included groundsheets, a thin waterproof layer of protection from the bare earth beneath. During the storm, rivulets of water began to trickle, then pour, then surge across the area on which the tents were pitched. The rain was so severe that, within a few minutes, Caroline's tent was lifted up on the swirling water gushing beneath. Without unzipping it, or venturing outside, she tried to adjust the floor, pushing against it with her forearm. Eventually the ferocity of the storm subsided, her tent settled back on the ground and she dozed off to sleep. She was then awoken by a sharp pain in her arm.

She tried to ignore it, but after five minutes she switched on her torch and saw two pinpricks in a swollen, red arm. She consoled herself with the thought that, as she puts it, "If it was a snake, you would no longer be sitting here, wondering if it were a snake; you would have been dead in five minutes. So, cool it, Cox, and wait until morning – it is only a scorpion, a spider, or a millipede." When daylight came, she made her way across the mud to a nearby village where a local doctor confirmed that she had indeed been bitten by a spider.

The incident – not the only life-threatening experience Caroline Cox has had in the field – left no permanent damage. But it raises an interesting question. Why would a dignified and highly intelligent woman in her middle years, daughter of a surgeon (who is still remembered as the author of an internationally renowned text on surgery) widow of a well-known psychiatrist and writer, nurse, mother of three, published author, and appointee to the House of Lords, choose to expose herself to dangerous aircraft and flight patterns, appalling insects and reptiles, arduous weather conditions, questionable food, death threats, and, on occasion, prison sentences, for offending brutal regimes?

Voice for the voiceless

Worlds away from the dangers of Sudan, on the banks of London's River Thames, the towers and spires of the Palace of Westminster rise in neo-Gothic splendour, marking the ancient home of the British Houses of Parliament. The palace's picture-postcard façade is crowned by the familiar presence of Big Ben, its great bell forever chiming the passing hours and minutes. Looking older than its years, much of the palace was rebuilt in the 1840s following a disastrous fire. However, some historic areas that survived the fire, such as the venerable Westminster Hall, have been in continuous use since the centre of government moved to Westminster in the eleventh century. Still today, ten centuries later, the two great parliamentary bodies of the United Kingdom's democracy – the House of Commons and the House of Lords – function inside the Palace of Westminster's walls.

The Lords Chamber is exceptionally ornate, richly decorated in gold and red. At one end is a throne, awaiting use by the reigning queen or king. For centuries, English monarchs have addressed the House's representatives to His or Her Majesty's Government from this throne, or one like it. Great Britain's history has rolled through the Houses of Parliament as the Thames rolls through England's countryside, in a never-ending flow: through war and peace; hope and despair; famine and plenty; and a monarchy at times beloved and, at times, berated.

During the twentieth century, the vast British empire, upon which the sun seemed never to have set, entered its twilight years. After the loss of a generation of young men in World War I and the life-or-death struggle against Hitler's Third Reich during World War II, Britain saw its power diminished, its role in world dominance reduced, and its influence eclipsed. Country after country around the globe, once shining stars in the British galaxy, gained independence.

Meanwhile, the Soviet Union, ally of the West during World War II, emerged as a threat to world freedom during the Cold War years. In the words of Sir Winston Churchill, "From Stettin in the Baltic to Trieste in the Adriatic, an iron curtain has descended across the Continent." The dramatic political shifts that took place during the twentieth century were marked by massive surges of violence and bloodshed. Pogroms behind that infamous Iron Curtain, Nazi genocide, Mao's conquest of China, and the subsequent Cultural Revolution, along with violence in Northern Ireland and the Middle East, added millions to the horrific body counts of the World Wars.

Throughout all these upheavals, the dismantling of the British empire and ever-shifting global allegiances, the British Parliament continued to uphold democracy, human rights, religious freedom, and Judeo-Christian values. In recent years, shifts in public opinion and a drive towards egalitarianism have caused changes in the way the peerage – membership in the House of Lords – is established. Today, the women and men who serve in the House of Lords are not entitled to their positions only by heredity; the vast majority are now there by appointment. Even as times change, however, and as debate continues about the composition of Parliament, nothing has been lost in the House of Lords' ambience. Authority and prestige still pervade the Lords Chamber, as in the rest of the Palace of Westminster, along with an unmistakable sense of history.

Today, Baroness Cox of Queensbury is a familiar face, having addressed the House of Lords for decades. Dark-haired, with clear eyes that miss nothing and a ready smile, she is a woman whose concerns, travels and activities are marked by youthful vigour. Her style of speech is quick and urgent. She is well known by those who serve alongside her as a champion of human rights, often addressing issues related to persecuted minorities around the world, and particularly Christians who cannot speak for themselves or whose voices are not heard.

It's true that Caroline had never envisioned herself actively engaged at the heart of Britain's Parliament. However, following her appointment it became evident that her family history – notably her father's dedication to medicine, which he practised well beyond Britain's borders – had prepared her for her new role in unanticipated and significant ways.

"My first real credential"

Robert John McNeill Love, a well-regarded surgeon who served in the Royal Army Medical Corps (RAMC) during World War I and as a civilian surgeon during World War II, would have been proud to hear of his only daughter's impressive position and laudable efforts. McNeill Love was a great hero in the eyes of many, including Caroline. And he forged a career path that she and her own children would eventually mirror, seamlessly interweaving the practical with the intellectual.

Robert McNeill Love's scholarly grasp of medicine and his skill as a surgeon provided the background necessary for his success as the author of *A Short Practice of Surgery*, which he co-authored with Hamilton Bailey. The book, which first appeared in 1932, was long the standard text for surgeons and is still in print.

It was not this book alone, however, that set McNeill Love apart from other medical professionals of his generation. His tireless work during World War I began in Turkey and moved into Mesopotamia following the bloodbath at Gallipoli. When the British Army appointed him as a goodwill ambassador, he began many a journey that took him from one obscure Arab village to another, tending to the medical needs of the poorest desert-dwellers.

A faded collection of sepia-tone photographs gathered in a family scrapbook reflects the stories McNeill Love later told about his odyssey. He described working all night aboard a Royal Navy hospital ship, performing forty amputations without anaesthetic, using hot tar to cauterise the stumps of limbs, staunching the flow of blood and providing an antiseptic barrier against deadly infections. He spoke of the Arab sheikhs he befriended. He wove tales about his travels among poor villages scattered along the ancient banks of the River Tigris.

Caroline remembers him describing a deadly outbreak of bubonic plague during 1917 and 1918. He was working in a remote desert township when he woke one morning to find himself surrounded by dying rats. In an attempt to stop the spread of the deadly disease he isolated the town – with himself inside – and tried to do what he could to alleviate the suffering. He never believed he would survive. Towards the end of the epidemic he received an urgent call from the local sheikh, asking him to come immediately: the sheikh's favourite wife had succumbed to the disease.

According to local belief, in order to go to heaven it was necessary to die in one's coffin. The lady was already prostrate and psychologically committed to dying. McNeill Love used all his newly learned Arabic trying to talk her out of the coffin – in vain. In desperation, he looked at his small supply of medicines and found the ideal, if unorthodox, remedy. He gave her a large dose of Epsom salts. Within ten minutes, she had leaped out of the coffin. And, as he said, she never looked back. The sheikh was so pleased that he offered Caroline's father any gift he would like, and

Robert McNeill Love became the owner of a magnificent Arab stallion.

McNeill Love served in the era of the crumbling Ottoman empire, the death march of 1,500,000 Armenians, the ravages of Gallipoli, and Britain's Mesopotamian campaign in today's Iraq. He had not yet married or established his family. He could never have imagined that all these tumultuous and historic events were setting the stage for his daughter's greatest challenges, both in the House of Lords and far beyond, more than half a century later.

Like her father, Caroline Anne McNeill Love – born in 1937, second child of Robert and his bright and gifted wife, Dorothy – pursued a health-service career, while at the same time publishing academically sound and widely respected books. Caroline says:

> *My first real credential is my father. I've seen his book in many parts of the world, in a remote clinic in Sudan and in a Turkish hospital in the Anatolian mountains. I've also found it on bookshelves in Surgeons' Quarters on board ships of the Royal Navy. He served in World War I, in the RAMC, which I gather has more Victoria Crosses than any other corps in the British Army. He spent most of the war in the Middle East, in Gallipoli and Mesopotamia. The fighting finished in that arena before the formal end of war; so he learned Arabic and was sent on many goodwill missions – a kind of medical Lawrence of Arabia. Perhaps my current lifestyle, spending much of my time in remote places, often in war zones, stems from stories heard as a child from my father.*

The rape of reason

In the early 1970s, Marxism was casting long shadows across the planet, and long-term fears of a Soviet invasion of Europe or a nuclear holocaust were punctuated by outbreaks of Marxist-based ideological vitriol and violence in universities and colleges. In the United States, the Vietnam War and the peace movement perpetuated well-publicised conflicts, epitomised by the tragic shootings at Kent State University, in May 1970. Similar encounters – not only anti-war, but anti-capitalist and anti-Western – were particularly endemic both in Britain and in Western Europe, especially West Germany.

In 1959, Caroline McNeill Love had married Dr Murray Cox, then a general medical practitioner who later specialised in psychiatry, working in a special hospital for patients who had committed crimes of violence and/or were a danger to themselves or others. He wrote highly acclaimed books that applied Shakespearean insights to psychiatric realities.

The Coxes' first son was born in November 1959. Less than a year later, the new wife and mother was admitted to Edgware General Hospital for six months, having been diagnosed with renal tuberculosis. Caroline Cox's time in hospital became a catalyst for her concerns about the humanising of nursing, about "treating a person with a disease, not a disease in a person". Some years later, this led to the publication of her widely read book *Sociology: An Introduction for Nurses, Midwives and Health Visitors* (1983).

After finally receiving a clean bill of health and the birth of her two other children, Caroline Cox completed her master's degree in sociology, and was offered a job as lecturer at the North Western Polytechnic, which, after a merger with another college, was renamed the Polytechnic of North London (PNL). In 1971 its faculty of 550 served 7,000 students. After a year, Cox moved up to the position of senior lecturer and was subsequently promoted to head of department. Serving in this capacity she encountered a dangerous faculty and student movement, composed of raging activists, some of whom had specifically enrolled at PNL in order to create a Marxist base.

In the years that followed, Caroline Cox endured personal attacks, assaults on her Christian faith, and accusations of fascism and incompetence. The years from 1971 to 1977 were marked by student protests, shouting matches in classrooms, disruption of college ceremonies, and widespread violence. On one occasion, her classroom was burst into by more than a dozen insurgents. Her chair was knocked over and she and her students were subjected to sustained, virulent verbal abuse. Their offence: holding a class on a day when the hard-line communist faculty and students, who had taken possession of the building, had decreed that no regularly scheduled classes should take place. There should be no exceptions to the "alternative education" that they had arranged, consisting of lectures on subjects including anti-American policies and "Marxism and the Third World".

Tactics against uncooperative academics such as Cox, including physical and psychological intimidation, lies, labelling, propaganda, and character assassination, were repeated exhaustively at the Polytechnic of North London. The department of which she was head consisted of twenty faculty members, sixteen of whom belonged to the Communist Party or other groups along the spectrum of Marxist-based ideologies and parties. Members of the faculty who did not compromise or conform to the will of the insurgency faced verbal abuse, physical threats, published libel, and public humiliation. Nothing was off-limits to the student movement. The cult-like demands of the communists even penetrated the seemingly sacred environs of family life, as illustrated by the experience of two of Caroline Cox's friends.

A young woman, previously one of Cox's students at another institution, had since married her boyfriend, who was on the academic staff at PNL. Cox recalls a frantic phone call from her former student, asking if they could meet as soon as possible.

Caroline found the young woman in tears, trying to understand why her husband, an active member of the Communist Party and a leader in the student upheaval at PNL, was about to abandon her. He had been advised by his cadre's leadership that either his wife must join the Party, or he would have to divorce her. His wife had refused to join.

The young man's hardened expression and unyielding position spoke volumes to Cox about the Marxists' mindset and the allegiance it demanded. His commitment to the Communist Party had to come first – before feelings, family loyalty, or the commitment he had made to his wife. Not only was the academic world a target, so was the traditional family. Aware as she was of the Marxists' malignant intentions, still Caroline Cox was stunned by their hardness of heart.

Caroline's father, Robert John McNeill Love, died in 1974. During a luncheon following the service of thanksgiving for his life, Caroline Cox was approached by a publisher, asking her to write what was to become a landmark book, *The Rape of Reason*, which described the Marxist domination of the Polytechnic of North London and the ideas that motivated it. The 1975 book opened doors for Cox that neither she nor anyone in her family could have either asked for or imagined.

In *The Rape of Reason* Caroline Cox and her co-authors, Keith Jacka and John Marks, wrote of the communist faculty and students' efforts: "The strategic aim is to destroy Western liberal democracy by totally discrediting its fundamental values of self-determination, respect for the rights of others, and the rule of law. What kind of society will follow is unclear, except that it will be minutely controlled (totalitarian) and will display a Marxist label."

In fact, the kind of society that would follow became all too clear to Cox in the years ahead. It was also clear to Bernard Levin, an influential columnist who was writing three articles a week in England's most prestigious newspaper *The Times*. On the morning before the book was to be published, Caroline was feeling nervous, realising she would face serious consequences at the Polytechnic for exposing the situation. She was hurriedly getting her children ready for school when the telephone rang. To her amazement it was Bernard Levin, whom she had never met. He explained that he had just read *The Rape of Reason*, and because he thought it was the most important book for the future of democracy that he had read in ten years, he was going to devote all three of that week's columns to it.

The initial article, published 30 September 1975, carried the eye-catching title, "In all its brutality, the making of an intellectual concentration camp". Levin wrote:

> ... I opened [the book] at random and within two
> minutes I had realised that it was a very serious
> work. Indeed, I read it through then and there
> and concluded it was one of the most serious
> books I had had in my hands for many years
> and that even more serious than the book itself
> and the appalling things it describes are its
> implications for our society as a whole... For four
> years the three authors and the other members
> of the academic and administrative staff with the
> necessary courage (both the moral and physical

kind were required continuously) fought against
the steady corruption of a place of learning
into something little better than an intellectual
concentration camp... I shall continue the subject
tomorrow...

A later article on 1 October concluded:

What exactly has happened at the Polytechnic
of North London? You can find out, in horrible
detail, by reading *Rape of Reason* and I hope
many people will. I can summarise it, however,
by saying that what has happened is that a few
people have determined to turn it into a place
where two do not necessarily make four, but
forty, or four hundred, or nineteen and a bit, if
they say so.

Yet Orwell was right: freedom is the freedom
to say that two plus two make four. And that is
why I do not much care if you do yawn when I
begin "Send not to ask for whom the bell tolls",
provided you realise that it may well be tolling,
at the Polytechnic of North London, for thee.

Bernard Levin's trilogy of articles made the book famous,
enhanced the reputation of the authors, and gave credibility
to their message. And, no doubt, it played a significant part in
the selection of Caroline Cox for appointment to the House
of Lords.

1979 – a revolutionary year

In 1977 Caroline Cox came to the conclusion that her efforts to stand up to the students at the Polytechnic of North London had continued long enough. Whatever purposes her tenacity and outspoken resistance had served, she had not succeeded in changing the ideological brainwashing that characterised so much of the sociology department's activities. She resigned her position as head of the department. Almost immediately she was offered a job at London University's Chelsea College as Director of the Nursing Education Research Unit. This new role promised to bring together her devotion to nursing as a compassionate vocation and her interest in ideas and academic work. It was not only a relief but a welcome new pathway – albeit one that would soon take some unexpected twists and turns.

Because of her role at Chelsea College, Cox, in 1979, was invited to travel to Turkey. The trip, sponsored by the prestigious British Council, was to provide a forum for dialogue between nursing colleges from the two countries, enabling them to discuss their common health issues and to develop nursing research. Incidentally, the visit also brought Caroline Cox amazingly close to her father's footsteps, where he had made his own medical journey – in Gallipoli and Mesopotamia.

Once she arrived in Istanbul, she found her surroundings fascinating – a skyline pierced with minarets; streets bustling with people in every sort of attire and lined with colourful wares. The city, an ancient crossroads between East and West, proved to be only an introduction to modern Turkey's cultural and political complexities, not to mention the dangerously backward sanitary conditions in some of the more remote areas. Perhaps most significantly the journey brought Caroline Cox face to face with the historical realities of the 1915–1923 Armenian genocide.

This massacre is denied to this day by the Turkish government, but was freely acknowledged by the Turkish nurses with whom Cox worked more than forty years ago. Two decades later, she would refer to this experience in the House of Lords:

> I hope passionately that Turkey will understand the damage being done to many of its own people by its attempts to continue to deny historical truth. Some years ago, I had the pleasure of visiting Turkey to undertake a professional programme of lectures on nursing and healthcare. I found many of my colleagues were fully aware of the genocide, freely admitted it and expressed their wish that their government would do so, so that they could live honestly with themselves as Turkish citizens and build good relations based on reconciliation with their Armenian neighbours. Until and unless the truth is recognised, the many decent, honest and principled people of Turkey will have to endure a schizophrenic existence to their own discomfort and at the cost of international peace and justice.
>
> **Hansard, 14 April 1999, vol. 599, col. 812**

The year of 1979 marked the broadening of Caroline Cox's world. Even as she moved steadily towards the international role that was yet to reveal itself, three world events transpired that year that would change her life and transform her world view.

In 1979, in the midst of grim economic forecasts and endless friction between government, trade unions, and industries, Margaret Thatcher became Great Britain's first female prime minister. Her mandate was to reduce the socialism that Conservatives thought was paralysing to the British economy. Like Cox, Thatcher was deeply critical of Marxism, communism, socialism, or any of their various permutations. And, like America's President Ronald Reagan, Thatcher took bold and controversial steps in economic restructuring and privatisation, while holding an uncompromising position in the face of Soviet aggression.

Later that year, next door to Turkey and seemingly light years away from Westminster, a religious and political drama was beginning to explode – its reverberations continue to shake the world even today. After the departure of the Shah of Iran, and following a national referendum, the highly regarded Shi'a religious leader, Ayatollah Khomeini, declared Iran an Islamic republic. Later in 1979, in the capital city of Tehran, Islamic militants seized the US embassy, taking sixty-six American diplomats and foreign service personnel captive. With Khomeini's apparent approval, the hostages were held for 444 days. This ordeal not only alienated the US from its former ally, Iran, but also broadcast angry images of Islamic fanaticism around the world.

Christmas Day 1979 marked yet another historical turning point. In an attempt to broaden its influence, protect the puppet communist government in Kabul, and insulate its territory, on 24 and 25 December, the USSR invaded Afghanistan, deploying more than 100,000 troops. The Afghans, who had been Muslim for centuries, fiercely retaliated, uniting their warlike tribes against a common enemy – the atheistic Soviets. The resistance fighters, taking the name "mujahedin", gained the respect and support of the Islamist world by declaring "jihad", or holy war, against their invaders. In the hope of overthrowing their arch-enemy the USSR, the United States began to support the mujahedin financially and militarily. Their mutual goal was accomplished more than ten years later – the Soviet Union was dissolved. Then the Islamic freedom fighters too quickly proved to be a formidable enemy in their own right, not only to the Soviets, but also to their Western benefactors.

Steps on a new pathway

For much of the world in the early 1980s, these events were eclipsed by the mundane realities of day-to-day survival. Even in great cities such as London and Washington DC, the implications of faraway battles seemed negligible. It would be years before Caroline Cox would find herself confronting jihadi warriors, or the victims left behind in their killing fields. Only after 11 September 2001 did the threat of militant Islam become a reality to most of the world.

The election of Margaret Thatcher as prime minister, however, became a turning point for Caroline Cox. Although she had never been political in her thinking (other than disappointing her father by not embracing his Conservativism), it was Mrs Thatcher's political concerns – primarily about education – that would place another key stepping stone on the pathway to Cox's most significant work.

During the early 1980s, Cox chaired the Centre for Policy Studies' (CPS) Education Study Group. This group, a think tank similar to America's Heritage Foundation, held annual meetings that were attended by Prime Minister Margaret Thatcher. After Mrs Thatcher had given a speech at one of these meetings, Cox was surprised and pleased to see her hold up a copy of Jacka, Marks, and Cox's *The Rape of Reason*, declaring to the audience, "If you haven't read this book, you should!"

She went on to provide a brilliant synopsis of the book's theme.

On a dark and drizzly Friday afternoon in mid-December 1982, Caroline was driving her car through London, barely moving as she passed the Palace of Westminster in heavy traffic. Glancing up at the Houses of Parliament, a random thought went through her mind: *What a pity there aren't more nurses in there*. She had long thought that too much money was being spent on high-end medical technology at the expense of hands-on nursing with its personal touch. Meanwhile, care for the elderly, the dying, the chronically sick, and the disabled was being diminished because of poor funding. It was a simple equation: cutbacks in nursing meant patients would suffer. And nurses' pay was pathetically inadequate. She had expressed her views forcibly and clearly in writing to her MP. Now, as the House of Lords receded in her rear-view mirror, she reflected sadly that she knew of only one nurse who was a peer in that noble institution, and there probably wouldn't be another in the foreseeable future.

That weekend she was preoccupied with putting the finishing touches to her textbook *Sociology for Nurses*. On Monday morning she dropped the manuscript off at publisher Butterworths, and, with a satisfying sense of finality, returned gratefully to her home and family. Now that she had finished her book, she told Murray and the family she was going to "cut out all the extras and just enjoy my job, my family and the simple life".

It was bliss. At Chelsea College the next day she felt completely relaxed. She returned home to an evening of shopping, cooking, and family life. As was her habit, she flicked through her telephone message book to see if she was needed to play a squash match for her team. It was then that she caught sight of a new note: "Please ring 10 Downing Street".

As it turned out, Caroline Cox's "simple life" had lasted all of twenty-two hours.

She was puzzled by the request but grateful that the caller had left the phone number, as it wasn't one she was likely to find in her address book. "I had no idea what it was about," she said later. She dialled the number, to be greeted by a well-modulated female voice: "Thank you for calling back. The Prime Minister wonders if you could possibly spare the time to call in and see her over the next few days."

"Of course," she responded, hoping her voice didn't betray the shock she was feeling. The woman enquired, "How about 4.45 tomorrow afternoon?" After agreeing on the time, Caroline tactfully enquired, "May I ask what this is regarding?" With the formidable presence of Margaret Thatcher looming large in her imagination, she added, "I don't mind coming with an open mind, but I'd rather not come with an *empty* mind!"

The refusal was polite, but emphatic. "I'm sorry; I have no further information for you. We look forward to seeing you at 4.45 tomorrow afternoon."

On 8 December 1982, upon first arriving at the historic home of Britain's prime ministers, Caroline apprehensively touched the doorbell on the black-panelled door, taking note of the brass number "10". Her heart was pounding. Once inside, she paced round a waiting room, occupying herself by examining the paintings. Before long the double doors swung open and a gentleman in formal attire announced, "The Prime Minister will see you now."

Taking a deep breath, she made her way through the portal. Margaret Thatcher thanked her warmly for coming, and said, "Please sit down. I'll come straight to the point, because I believe in coming straight to the point. I've read some of your books on education and I'm preparing a list of names to give to Her

Majesty the Queen for recommendations for life peerages. May I put your name on that list?"

Caroline was stunned. She'd had no inkling this could be the purpose of the meeting – not in her grandest dreams. She had no active involvement in politics, and was not, in fact, even a member of the Conservative Party. Nonetheless, Mrs Thatcher made it perfectly clear that, having read some of Caroline Cox's writings about education, she intended to appoint her to the House of Lords. And Thatcher was very fair, saying that she hoped Caroline would support her party on education, but she knew Caroline did not always agree with the Conservatives' health policy. So she reassured her, "You always have the freedom to speak and to vote according to your conscience."

For a woman with no political aspirations or parliamentary ambitions it was a breathtaking moment – unexpected and unsolicited. She had rehearsed no response. Her sense of trepidation was profound, but so was her respect for both the opportunity and the woman who had offered it to her. In the days that followed, she chose the title Baroness Cox of Queensbury, finding herself, as she often describes it now, "a nurse by intention and a baroness by astonishment".

Solidarity with the Polish people

The communist-inspired uprisings at the Polytechnic of North London had provided Caroline Cox with an exceptionally close look at the ideological belief system of Marxism and its adherents' attempts to transform the world in their image. She assumed she had seen more than her fair share of Marxism by the time she left PNL and moved on to Chelsea College. In fact, no matter how instructive, it had been only the briefest introduction. Disturbing, degrading, and at times brutal as the confrontations at PNL may have been, Caroline Cox was about to see the communist system at work more closely than she ever had before, and in a far more virulent form.

In an article published in *World Magazine* on 11 December 2004 Mindy Belz wrote:

> Having accurately characterized the problems with Marxism, she set about to help its victims behind the Iron Curtain. She signed on as a patron of the Medical Aid for Poland Fund. The work took her across Europe for weeks at a time, eating and sleeping out of delivery trucks as the relief group brought medicine and other supplies to the dispossessed in Poland, Romania, and Russia.

Five years after leaving the chaotic environment of the Polytechnic of North London, Caroline Cox was, in June 1982, making her way across Europe in a rattling 32-tonne supply truck, heading for the infamous border that then separated East from West. After nine hours of exhausting searches by unsmiling border officials, she and the driver eventually passed the heavily guarded checkpoints and navigated the big vehicle through poorly lit, poverty-stricken Polish streets. There Caroline Cox became an eyewitness to a world governed by the ideas that PNL's faculty and students had so aggressively promoted during their "occupation". Their tactics – intimidation, abuse, character assassination, twisted truths, and blatant lies had been applied unmercifully in the Eastern bloc, enforced by totalitarian leaders against those who refused to submit to their claims or surrender to their authority.

In 1983, Baroness Cox of Queensbury began to meet dissidents, one by one, many of whom were devout Christians who would become prisoners of conscience in Poland, Romania, and the Soviet Union. She visited their homes. She listened to their stories. Later she watched from afar, taking note as those dissidents' faith, their devotion to family and their fierce commitment to truth was tested by the force of the fist, the barrel of a gun, or the torturer's cell. She was grieved. She was enraged. She began to speak on their behalf.

Chapter Two

Poland, Romania, Russia –
The Iron Hand of Communism

Beneath a pale sky on 8 April 2005, St Peter's Square in Vatican City was a sea of grey, black, and cardinal red. The air was filled with the quiet murmur of voices and the flutter of pigeon wings. As if searching for words of hope, a persistent wind moved across the pages of the Holy Gospel, which rested on top of the simple wooden coffin.

In the days surrounding the funeral of Pope John Paul II, Rome's streets and avenues teemed with pilgrims. In fact, according to the *The Guardian* on 9 April 2005, an estimated two million had travelled from Poland, determined to pay their final respects to the world's first Polish pope, former Krakow priest Karol Wojtyla.

During his pontificate, John Paul II had spoken words of courage, faith, and love to countless lands, in innumerable languages. But he had left behind a specific legacy in his beloved homeland. And the Poles remembered. Like most of Eastern Europe, since the end of World War II and the Yalta Treaty, Poland had been clenched within the iron fist of Soviet authority. Personal freedom, truth, and justice vanished; food was scarce; and opportunity for change was apparently non-existent.

Then came 2 June 1979, when the Polish pope returned to his homeland, kissed the soil on arrival, and declared a message that reverberated with hope. Papal biographer George Weigel describes the scene:

> Rebuilt Warsaw was a grim, gray place, its skyline dominated by the Palace of Culture and Sciences, a garish communist-baroque confection given to the city by Stalin. The city's grayness too often matched the people's mood. Now, for the Pope, Warsaw had come alive, visually and spiritually. Thousands of pilgrims had been welcomed into the homes of strangers. Every church in the city had remained open overnight to give shelter to those who could not find places elsewhere....
>
> The city had been transformed by homemade decorations. The windows and porches of the drab apartment blocks along the roads John Paul would travel had been turned into shrines and altars bedecked with flowers, flags and photographs of the Pope. As the papal motorcade moved slowly along the street, bouquets were thrown in the Pope's path while the crowd broke out in songs, cheers, and, in some cases, uncontrollable tears...

Weigel goes on to record Pope John Paul's words to his fellow countrymen and women on the last day of his pilgrimage:

> You must be strong, dear brothers and sisters.... You must be strong with the strength of *faith*...

Today more than in any other age you need this strength. You must be strong with the strength of *hope*, hope that brings the perfect joy of life and doesn't not allow us to grieve the Holy Spirit.

You must be strong with *love*, which is stronger than death...

So... I beg you: never lose your trust, do not be defeated, do not be discouraged... I beg you: have trust, and... always seek spiritual power from Him from whom countless generations of our fathers and mothers have found it. Never detach yourselves from Him. Never lose your spiritual freedom.

from *Witness to Hope* (London: HarperCollins, 1995)

Poland: light in the darkness

As we have seen, 1979 was a year of beginnings – for better or worse. In 1979, Pope John Paul II made his first visit to Poland following his investiture, and this marked yet another change, although it was a change that was slowly kindled. His visit sparked the fire of *Solidarnosc* – Solidarity, the trade union founded by Lech Walesa (who was later to receive the Nobel Peace Prize). Solidarity's defiant dock strikes, Walesa's imprisonment, the indomitable spirit and support of the Polish people, and relentless pressure from the Vatican eventually led to the downfall of the communist regime's "culture of the lie" in Poland. The decade that followed the Holy Father's visit was marked with violent upheaval and stubborn resistance.

It was during that decade, four years after the Pope's groundbreaking visit to Poland, that Caroline Cox also became involved with Poland's struggle for freedom. In 1983, as a member of the House of Lords, she was invited to serve as a patron of Medical Aid for Poland, an organisation that had been set up in response to an urgent plea from Lech Walesa. Medical Aid for Poland's mission was to procure and deliver such key medical needs as needles, syringes, bandages, intravenous fluids, catheters, basic medicines, anaesthetics, and baby formula. Money was collected, necessary products were either purchased or donated, and the cargo was transported by lorry across Europe into Poland. A few weeks after agreeing to serve as a patron, Caroline Cox suggested that she would like to travel occasionally with the delivery trucks into Poland. "I asked to do so for two reasons," she recalls with a flash of defiance. "First, to ensure they got through to where they were most needed; and also to be able to say 'I have been, I have seen, and this is how it really is.'"

Here were sown the seeds of principles that have undergirded all of Caroline Cox's humanitarian endeavours, which, she explains,

> *are based on the foundations of four "As": Aid for forgotten and neglected people often trapped behind closed borders, frequently not served by major aid organisations for security or political reasons; Advocacy for oppressed and persecuted people; Accountability to those for whom we speak, that our message is accurate and sensitive – and also accountability to supporters that they know what we have done and what they have made possible; and Authenticity, based on personal visits to obtain first-hand evidence for purposes of advocacy and the appropriate use of aid.*

Over the next eight years there would be twelve trips to affirm those principles. Some took place in the dead of winter; all of them were journeys into the eerie world of totalitarian control. During those visits, Cox saw the communistic ideas and ideals once so enthusiastically promoted at the Polytechnic of North London now threatening to stifle Poland's spiritual, intellectual, and national impulses as well as the very lives of the Polish people. The system was indefensible, and would eventually crumble. And the Poles who stood against it were unforgettably courageous and sacrificial – taking risks as if they had no alternative.

The man with the black satchel

Baroness Cox recalls, "Anyone who visited Poland in those dark, dark days of communism and martial law will tell you that fear was tangible the moment you crossed the Iron Curtain. There were tanks, there were watchtowers with the guns pointing inward, there were dogs. You felt yourself in a vast prison of free spirits." One senses, as she speaks, that her outrage toward the Marxist system contributed to her desire not only to aid the people of Poland, but to challenge the system that oppressed them.

The secret police system was indeed ubiquitous – tapping phones, stalking, intimidating, and at times detaining and arresting those who stepped beyond the boundaries the state would tolerate. On one early trip, Caroline Cox found herself trailed by a man, clearly a secret policeman, who appeared just as she boarded a train for Warsaw, and who waited uneasily for it to leave the station. Although she described it light-heartedly to her friends, she was terrified by the experience.

In the following excerpts from his book *Baroness Cox: A Voice for the Voiceless*, Andrew Boyd describes the incident involving the man she dubbed "Black Satchel":

> Surrounded by an ever-growing crowd, she suddenly noticed a man on the platform with a black satchel who was staring at her. She told herself not to be so paranoid; it was only a coincidence.
>
> Time passed and still the train refused to budge from the platform as more and more passengers piled on. "Black Satchel" was still there, staring, and she thought, "Okay, Caroline Cox, you're not that attractive; maybe it is the secret police. If so, so what? There nothing to be ashamed of or to worry about."
>
> Black Satchel... was a weaselly, cadaverous-looking figure, clad in a leather jacket, and standing too close for comfort...
>
> Suddenly she remembered her growing collection of Solidarity badges – the little red and white metal enamel badges had been showered on her at the various places she had visited. Each bore the crest of a local organization, which would both chart her visit and incriminate those she had met. She swallowed hard and composed herself, trying to maintain her sang-froid for the sake of Black Satchel...
>
> The train had been standing at the platform for almost an hour and still showed no sign of moving, so she thought maybe she should get off and try to find her way back to her friends. But

just as she was about to step off, it jolted forward and began to gather momentum...

Taking her leave from Black Satchel she made her way into a compartment with four other passengers, one in each corner. That left two seats on either side in the centre. Caroline took one; Black Satchel quickly took the other. He parked himself down, knee-to-knee, still staring.

His secret service credentials were ratified immediately by the reaction of the other passengers. They all studiously avoided Caroline's eyes.

She extricated a fat novel from her rucksack and started to read it... After some three hours with Black Satchel staring at her book cover [by coincidence called *Don't Look Now*!] and she staring equally hard at the pages, at the next station Black Satchel got off. Caroline presumed the train had reached the end of his jurisdiction. She realized Black Satchel would not have invested so much in following her that far, without having someone else to take his place.

She scrutinized the oncoming passengers to try to pinpoint her new minder. It wasn't difficult. He marched straight into the compartment. He was conspicuous by his clothing, which was well beyond the pocket of ordinary Polish people. To double-check, Caroline stepped out of the carriage. Immediately he followed her, placed himself right next to her and started talking to her in English. She thought, *Thank you for making it so obvious.*

The rest of the journey became a battle of wits. He would fire questions at her to try to trap her into saying something inappropriate, something that would get her into trouble. His opening gambit was to ask for her views on Communism. What he lacked in subtlety, he made up for in persistence. She would evade his questions and try to trap him into divulging who he really was. It was as good a game as any to while away the journey.

When they got off the train, Caroline searched for ways to shake off her unwanted chaperone. Black Satchel had looked unfit and easy to outrun. This one was younger, leaner and an altogether more difficult proposition. Caroline did her fair share of ducking and weaving and back-tracking to try to throw him off the scent. Moving as quickly as she could, she melded with the crowds on the platform until she could no longer see him. Realizing that didn't mean he could no longer see her, she took a number of detours up and down flights of stairs. She was to be met at the station and was eager to shrug him off before he could catch sight of her contact. Though with that degree of surveillance his employers were probably well aware of where she was staying and with whom. As she was to find out.

The secret police continued to let Caroline Cox and her Polish friends know that they were always around, always conscious of her movements. A woman name Lidia, who was often Cox's host in Poland, never received the letters Caroline sent in advance of her arrival. These letters were meant to inform Lidia of Cox's itinerary and to provide information about her visit. Rather than delivering them in a timely manner, the state placed them all in Lidia's mailbox at the same time – always on the precise day of Lady Cox's appearance. That was just one way the authorities revealed their awareness of everything that was happening – it was a practised policy of menace and intimidation.

Lidia, who had few financial resources, was thrown into a frantic search for food and other necessities, searching in shops that were constantly empty except for bottles of pickled gherkins and vodka. Even after standing for hours in line she was unable to provide the kind of generous hospitality for her guest that she desired. In Cox's view, the hospitality of the Polish people was both inspiring and humbling in that they never revealed to their guests the sacrifices behind the meals they so enthusiastically prepared.

Baroness Cox was also welcomed on frequent occasions by a Catholic priest, Father Alexander Chycki, who frequently expressed his warm appreciation whenever she arrived on one of the Medical Aid lorries. With the help of local seminarians, he assisted in unloading the trucks himself and also lent a hand in the distribution of supplies. Invariably the secret police were close at hand.

Lady Cox describes one typical incident.

> *I usually slept in the truck, on the narrow top bunk of the cab with the truck driver below, often chain smoking all night long. But on one occasion Father Chycki arranged for me to stay overnight in an apartment. I had just taken my rucksack inside when there was a knock on the door and these two guys came bursting in. "We've just come to fix a light*

bulb," they explained, clearly intending to bug the place. I thought, "If it's anything it's not subtle!"

She recounts one conversation with Father Chycki:

He wanted to talk, so we went out and sat in his car, which he parked in the middle of nowhere away from the ubiquitous bugging devices. And what he said to me really gave me new insight into the nature of communist totalitarianism. He said that one of the things that grieved him most was that it was impossible either to conceptualise or to implement the concept of charity, or caritas, in a communist context because, of course, in the ideology of communism the state provides everything, so no one is in need.

It's no accident that in totalitarian societies such as communism, one of the first things they do is destroy any non-government organisations – youth movements, girl scouts – or they take them over. The state provides everything so there's no opportunity to develop private initiatives or caritas. Father Chycki said that he found this saddening because as he was trying to teach his congregation about the concept of charity, there was no practical way to exercise it. He explained that this was one of the most deadening effects of communist regimes because it destroys the soul by destroying the opportunity for the expression of charitable love.

"I believe in love"

Despite the state's attempts to extinguish charity, the Polish people persisted in their efforts to help those in need. No one needed help more than the children. And as Lady Cox likes to point out, it is the hope in the hearts of children that seems to light the darkest corners of the world. Andrew Boyd describes a discovery Caroline Cox made in a children's hospital.

The courage of the Poles was also apparent in the children's hospital in the historic city of Krakow. What was once a dignified building was a run-down structure of bleak staircases and bare concrete floors. At least it was clean, which Caroline noted was no mean achievement, given the chronic lack of soaps and detergents.

On one ward were children with malignant diseases. Many had the kind of leukaemia which would be treatable in the UK. The doctors and nurses were well aware that it could be cured, but they had only a fraction of the resources necessary to treat it. So they faced the agonizing decision of choosing which child to treat, and which to leave. Those who were left had little hope. Those who were treated faced an ordeal. The treatment involved intravenous injections at four-hourly intervals. Pediatric-sized needles were a rarity, so nursing staff would have to use large-bore items intended for adults. "It might take hours, literally, to try to get one of those big needles into these little children's veins."

Caroline talked to some parents about the courage of the children she saw in those wards.

They told her the story of a 12-year-old boy in the Warsaw uprising. The fighting was at its height, tanks were approaching, they were under constant bombardment and people were dying all around. With his own death imminent, the boy wrote these words on a wall: "I believe in the sun, even when I cannot see it. I believe in love, even when I cannot feel it."

Perhaps it is not surprising, in the light of such vibrant faith, that John Paul II's visit to Poland was empowering. In the spiritual vacuum of Marxism, it was the devoutly Catholic country of Poland that seemed best equipped to face oppression with Christian characteristics such as truth, courage, love, and patience. During the most hopeless days, when all seemed lost, Caroline Cox was astonished to see the churches there filled to overflowing with people.

One morning was bitterly cold, with ice and snow outside. I think we went to the eight o'clock mass. As we arrived, people were pouring out from the seven o'clock mass. We later learned that the six o'clock mass had been equally full. When we finished the eight o'clock mass, people were queuing and crowding outside to get into the nine o'clock mass. There would be three more masses that day, and they would all be equally full. This was a suburban Catholic church and not one of the big cathedrals – a local Catholic church and a local community. And people weren't there for show. They were really worshipping. We know this because of what it cost them. Just as is it today in so many places around the world, they knew

that if they went to church, then they'd be much
less likely to get a job, or their kids would be denied
entry into a university, or they would face arrest
and imprisonment. Yet they exercised real faith,
dedication, and, in the service, real worship.

The work Caroline Cox accomplished during her years as patron of Medical Aid for Poland was instructive preparation for innumerable future trips spanning three decades to more countries than she can readily recall. Not only did she work to help provide the donated supplies and cash necessary for the project, but she also used her personal hands-on experience with the beleaguered Polish people as the focal point of her efforts in the House of Lords to provide practical assistance for them.

On 11 December 1989, she voiced a parliamentary question, quoted in Hansard, regarding "Poland's Medical and Environmental Aid". Here are some excerpts from her statement:

My Lords, I am very grateful for this opportunity
to raise matters which I believe are of the utmost
importance not only for Poland but for the other
emerging democracies in Eastern Europe, for
Europe as a whole and for the future of freedom
and democracy. I am also grateful to the other
noble Lords who will be contributing to this
debate...

Your Lordships may be aware that last week
I was travelling to Poland with a 32-tonne truck
full of medical supplies. As a scene-setter to
this debate I should like to invite your Lordships
to accompany me in imagination to two of the
places I visited. I shall then provide some of

the latest statistics which portray the larger
picture behind the individual examples of human
suffering, statistics which demonstrate the
catastrophic proportions of Poland's problems.
I will conclude by urging the government
to respond much more urgently and more
appropriately to the desperate needs of the
Polish people.

Hansard, 11 December 1989, vol. 513, cols. 1180–81

After describing the needs of one children's hospital in an industrial city, and its specific shortages relating to the treatment of leukaemia through intravenous injections, which resulted "not only in suffering but in unnecessary death", she continued:

Now please would you accompany me in
imagination to one of the hospitals I visited in
Warsaw last week? It is a typical hospital. The
corridor in the cardiac unit is full of beds with
seriously ill people lying amidst a constant flow
of people and trolleys, surrounded by noise, with
complete lack of privacy. This is because Warsaw
can only provide care in coronary care units for
a mere 40 to 50 per cent of patients suffering
from heart attacks. Many just therefore risk death
being cared for in those noisy corridors...
    Coronary heart disease is the biggest
health problem in Poland today, accounting for
approximately 51 per cent of deaths. It is killing
more and more people at younger and younger

ages, with the highest mortality in the world for middle-aged men. Many could be effectively treated by surgery, such as coronary bypass. But Poland can only provide for 10 per cent – 10 per cent! – of those who need this life-saving treatment. So very many people, including many who are relatively young and could enjoy many more years of healthy life, will die unnecessarily.

Hansard, 11 December 1989, vol. 513, cols. 1180–81

On this occasion, Baroness Cox appealed to the British government for several specific kinds of help. With precision she pointed out that she had had personal meetings with members of the Polish parliament, including some very senior ministers. Just over a month later, on 16 January 1990, she met Prime Minister Margaret Thatcher to address the same subjects. Two weeks after this meeting, on 1 February, Mrs Thatcher personally responded with a four-page letter, addressing and responding to Lady Cox's requests one by one.

Sharing the darkness

In Poland, she first came face to face with the cruel effects of oppression on daily life: fear, despair, and hunger. And yet she often saw these painful feelings counterbalanced by courage, hope, and generosity.

During one trip to Poland, she and her truck driver, Tony, a big cockney man from East London with an even bigger heart, sat down to a meal prepared by their Polish hosts. Unless they were Communist Party members, the Poles had little food. "For all the years I went I hardly ever saw good quality fresh fruit available for ordinary people," Caroline Cox recalls. "It was in the Party's shops, but nowhere else. I remember seeing only one fresh lemon. It was on a Warsaw market stall. We worked out the price at twelve pounds sterling."

One of the church members nurtured a small garden of strawberries. At that dinner, all the strawberries she had grown were distributed among the guests – the British lorry driver and Lady Cox. "I felt really bad about eating them," she said. "I wanted to refuse but it was their dignity and their pride to give us their best."

Later, as Tony and Caroline drove away, she was reorganising the lorry's cab. She reached under the seat and noticed a paper bag there. Looking inside, she discovered that it was filled with strawberries. As if they hadn't given enough already, their Polish hosts had hidden away one more expression of their never-ending hospitality. Feeling close to tears, Caroline said to Tony, "How can we even begin to describe what it's like in Poland? How can we make people understand how poor the Polish people are and yet how generously they give?"

Tony was choked up too. In his cockney accent he replied, "All I ever say is, 'They've got nuffink, and they give you everyfink.'"

Andrew Boyd describes her last trip to Poland before the end of the communist regime.

The truck driver had taken a particularly circuitous route and ground to a halt in the middle of a forest in the small hours of the morning. Whether or not they had broken down Caroline couldn't say because the driver was Polish and the limits of conversation were prescribed by their mutual ability to mime.

His abilities were limited. He had gone off for purposes of his own and Caroline was left alone. It was pitch dark.

Driven by her normal, frantic schedule Caroline often found it difficult to make time to stop and meditate on her faith, although she appreciated moments when she could "be still and know that I am God". Now she was sitting in a cramped, uncomfortable truck in the middle of the night, in the middle of a Polish forest in the middle of nowhere. And she thought, I have no reason whatsoever not to use this time to meditate. Trying to still her anxiety, she committed the time to God and asked him to help her listen to his word and respond. It took a while to calm her thoughts. "Then the words just came into my mind," she said later, "and they have stayed with me to this day. They were: 'Share the darkness.'"

On 6 November 1990, Caroline Cox returned to a free Poland. She had received an invitation to go to the Parliament building to see the new democracy in action. While she was there, one of the Polish parliamentarians thanked her for all she had done for Poland during their dark days. He then said, "And we thank you for sharing our darkness." Caroline caught her breath, remembering how those same words had come to her during her time alone with God. Not long afterwards, she was awarded the highest honour Poland offers to a foreigner – the Commander's Cross of the Order of Merit of the Republic of Poland.

Child of Romania

In her many journeys to Poland, Lady Cox encountered Poland's unique spirituality, burning like a candle that never sputtered out, casting broad light into a shadowy culture of deceit, duplicity, and death. Poland was, in a spiritual sense, unique. It shone in dramatic contrast to the darkness that fell over Romania during its years as a Marxist regime. Ruled by the despot Nicolae Ceausescu, Romania set its own course as a brutal police state, even resisting the Soviet Union's policies in a number of ways, promoting instead Ceausescu's own egotistical and nationalistic version of Marxism-Leninism.

In 1967 Ceausescu became supreme leader of Romania. His rule was marked by disastrous economic schemes that led to repressive and corrupt practices, exceptional even in the days of the Iron Curtain. Tight rationing led to near-starvation, which affected much of the population. Meanwhile, an Orwellian birth policy, intended to boost the population, made it the duty of every woman to produce at least five children. As a result, there were more hungry mouths to feed than there was food, and innumerable state-run orphanages, filthy and impoverished, overflowed with unwanted children.

Predictably, within a tightly controlled media, the daily newspaper of the Party, *Scinteia*, reported nothing but praise for Ceausescu. And, thanks to *Securitate*, the dictator's notorious secret police network that managed to place informers even within immediate families, there was virtually no dissent.

Romania was constricted by Ceausescu's stranglehold for nearly twenty years, but as with many other Marxist regimes of the day, release came at last. In December 1989, a popular uprising, which was quickly joined and supported by the army, led to the arrest and execution of Nicolae Ceausescu and his wife, Elena. Even then, the people who had fought against all odds for their freedom faced a great struggle. Once the borders were opened, and indeed for years afterwards, Romania's poverty shocked the world.

In 1990, Caroline Cox visited Romania for the first time, focusing as she often did on orphanages, hospitals, and other healthcare facilities. Conditions in state-run institutions had been bad enough in Poland; the state of affairs in Romania was deplorable. Orphaned and abandoned children lived in harsh, cold squalor, evident from the abuse of their bodies and their depression. Scenes of neglect and stories of abandonment were endemic wherever she went.

Yet in one orphanage, a typically inhospitable facility, there was another unexpected spark of hope. There Caroline Cox met a young girl named Dorina who was only twelve years old – bright, friendly, and caring about the other children around her. It wasn't long before the Romanian orphan had befriended the English baroness. Lady Cox was surprised to learn that Dorina had taught herself English and could already make herself understood when speaking. She felt an immediate bond with Dorina, and was moved to tears by her circumstances.

"Later, when I came back to Britain," Caroline Cox explains, "I kept in touch with Dorina because I couldn't forget her – she was just so impressive, a very special little girl. And I used to write to her and send her books in English to encourage her English speaking. We did that for quite a few years. Then I heard that she had managed to get a scholarship to study social work." She continues:

> *I was able to facilitate her coming over to Britain,*
> *and I'll never forget meeting Dorina again. I'd*
> *always seen her as this rather vulnerable little*

girl, impressive, gracious, but very poignant in
this orphanage in Romania. And here was a very
attractive, slight but mature and gracious young
lady. I was just so moved to see her.

What she brought over was particularly
poignant to me: a notebook of all the letters I had
sent her over those years. Everything I'd sent her was
all in this notebook. And then, obviously, she came
with very few clothes, really nothing for the very
harsh English winter. And so I took her shopping.
It was so touching because she said to me part way
through our time together when we were shopping,
"This is the first time in my life anyone has ever
taken me shopping. In the orphanage we just all had
standard orphan clothes, so I've never actually been
shopping with anyone in my life."

Today Dorina Maguran is married and lives with her husband
Tavi and her son, Nicholas, in Oxford, England. She writes of
her difficult early life and her transformative friendship with
Baroness Cox:

I was born on the 16th of November 1978 in a town
called Gurahont in the city of Arad – Romania. My
parents lived together for a few months after I was
born and then separated; they were never married
and were living in poverty. They both had alcohol
problems. This was not the right environment to
bring up a child and they were not responsible
parents. My mother abandoned me when I was
born and my grandmother looked after me for six
years. My mother visited me at my grandmother's

but never wanted me to live with her. When I was seven my grandmother was too old to look after me so the Local Authorities sent me to an orphanage in Arad where I stayed for eleven years.

The orphanage was a terrible place, it was a very old building, damp, and cold, gloomy and the men and women looking after us were extremely strict.

After the Communist regime ended, many people from different countries used to come to visit Romanian orphanages. One of these people marked my future and helped me to be where I am today. It was 1990 and there were about one hundred children living in the orphanage where I grew up. One summer's afternoon our carers told us that somebody was coming to visit us. We were all very happy and waited all afternoon in the main hall to see who the visitors would be. Late in the evening the door opened and Lady Cox together with some other people came in. They were carrying lots of boxes with clothes and food in small boxes and big boxes, and the big room soon was full to the ceiling.

Some of the children jumped into our lovely visitors' arms to get a hug from them. Although it was a normal feeling to wish to be loved in a place like this, I was feeling embarrassed to do this. Some children asked me to translate for them things like: "I want up in your arms" or "How are you, tell me more about you..."

Lady Cox saw me and heard me speaking in English; she came to me with her lovely angelic smile to ask some questions. She asked me my name, how old I was and where I had learned to speak English...

I felt really happy... answering their questions about me. More children came around and I remember one of the carers saying with a loud voice: "Don't stay so close to Lady Cox she is a baroness so move." The carer didn't speak English at all so our visitors didn't understand her. It was only then that I found out that Lady Cox is a baroness and I began being nervous talking to her.

Lady Cox asked me if I like reading and she said that she would send me books to improve my English. I was so happy when she gave me her address and asked for mine. She said that she would like to correspond with me. I remember her going to our medical cabinet and writing a list of the medicines needed for the children. Lady Cox gave me a hug and then they left. That evening I went to sleep really happy.

Shortly after this I was really surprised to receive letters and books from her. The first parcel contained easy story books, then harder ones such as Enid Blyton, *The Wind in the Willows*, and big hard glossy book called *The Beauty of Britain*. I read them all very studiously in order to improve my English. She also sent me photographs of her family and a picture on which she had written, "This is our house from the country, and we hope you will visit us one day."

I replied to all Lady Cox's letters and told her all about school and life in the orphanage... we

began our correspondence in December 1990
and I have kept all the letters I have received
from her. They are very precious to me.

After obtaining my degree in social work I
began working for the Child Protection Authority
in Romania where I remained for almost three
years. I wrote to Lady Cox to ask if there was any
possibility for me to come to England, because
the British system is very advanced in the social
work area. I felt that the experience I would gain
in England would be very valuable in my own
country. Lady Cox agreed and very kindly made
arrangements for me to come to England...

After the fall of the Ceausescu regime, Baroness Cox was
invited to be an observer of the Romanian elections. Of that
experience, she recalls,

> *What was interesting was, again, Romania's*
> *atmosphere was very different from Poland's.*
> *The Polish elections were very good because the*
> *people had come through with their integrity*
> *uncompromised. Deeply and passionately*
> *committed to democracy, the Poles were able to*
> *preserve the fundamentals of democracy. Romania*
> *had been much more compromised. There was*
> *corruption throughout – endemic – and the*
> *elections, we had to say, were not free and fair. There*
> *was a lot of manipulation in the media beforehand*
> *and there was a lot of intimidation from the*
> *old communist thugs. Romania's was a totally*
> *different atmosphere from Poland's – if you went*

in blind and you opened your eyes and found
yourself in Poland, you'd be breathing different
air than if you were blind and opened your eyes in
Romania. I think it's probably like this even in the
present day.

Russia: trajectories of despair

During Caroline Cox's first journeys into restricted countries
in the 1980s and 1990s, her response to displaced, deprived,
and dejected children became a focus of her work, and remains
so to this day. Her introductory visit to the former USSR,
however, concerned other matters. She went to Moscow in
1988 at the invitation of Valery Senderov, a well-known Russian
Orthodox mathematician who had spent many years in the
harsh conditions of Stalin's camps in the infamous gulags. He
and several other dissidents had planned a press conference
to publicise their intolerable circumstances under Soviet rule.
Senderov depicted life under the authority of the USSR's
political system as a form of imprisonment. "In the Bible we
are exhorted to visit those in prison," he pleaded in a video
smuggled out to the West. "We are in this huge prison; please
will you come and visit us?"

"Senderov's invitation wasn't one I could say no to," Caroline
explained later. But saying yes would involve substantial risks.
Technically, holding such a conference could be classified as
subversion under the Soviet constitution. Still, she was fairly
sure that if they held the press conference and she got out of the
country immediately afterwards, it would be safe. Any decision
to arrest a British parliamentarian would have to be passed all
the way to the top of the politburo and down again. By the time

the Soviet bureaucracy had made up its mind to arrest her she would be out of harm's way.

Caroline went into Russia on a Thomas Cook tour. Joining her on the long-weekend package holiday was Malcolm Pearson, later Lord Pearson of Rannoch, who had agreed to accompany her. They had met during her Polytechnic years, and he shared her concerns about the Marxists in higher education. But their sense of a common cause ran deeper. "Malcolm has this strong commitment to resist what he perceives as evil," Cox says, "and he always saw Soviet Communism as one of the great evils in the contemporary world." Lord Pearson had been raising money for the dissident networks, and Aleksandr Solzhenitsyn had stayed in Malcolm's Scottish home when he came to Britain to receive the Templeton Award for Religion in 1983.

Flying into Moscow, Caroline and Malcolm first caught sight of the tall, drab apartment buildings that loomed for miles and miles around Sheremetyevo airport. Inside their weather-beaten cement walls were warehoused – in poverty and fear – untold thousands of Russian families. To the alert Westerner, those endless blocks of apartments represented the abject desolation that had spread, like a deadly disease, across Russia's 10 million square miles.

Russia was a land whose religious faith and rich culture had for centuries throbbed with liveliness and beauty. Russian music, literature, and ballet had long illuminated the world with artistic passion and perfection. Now, behind the vast confines of the Iron Curtain, daily life had been reduced to a grim, monochromatic struggle for survival. Families with several children were crammed into one-room apartments with no privacy and inadequate sanitation. Even the most basic foods were rationed, requiring everyone – young, old, sick, or crippled – to stand in interminable food queues.

Throughout Russia, since the Bolshevik Revolution, the simplest joys of life had been sacrificed to the state, and hope had been forfeited to mind-numbing despair. It was the era of glasnost and perestroika. Many of the Soviet Union's senior dissidents had been freed from the prison camps of the infamous gulag. But KGB pressure was mounting; there was renewed harassment, and fears that the cold grip of totalitarianism was about to clamp down again.

Under watchful eyes

Despite glasnost – or perhaps because of it – the KGB was still very active. Caroline and Malcolm would need to take elaborate precautions over meeting their contacts. They checked into their hotel, a vast Stalinist edifice, and met their contact and interpreter, Vera, as prearranged. Their rooms were dark and grubby and in all probability bugged, so they kept their conversation to trivialities, or communicated by notes.

On the first morning they broke loose from their tour group and tried to get to a telephone. The air was bitterly cold and the pavements were dangerously icy. Walking was impossible. They hailed a taxi, a large black Volga. That was when they had their first open encounter with the KGB.

An enormous man tried to squeeze into the Volga with Caroline. "He was a typical caricature of a KGB thug: large, raincoat, fur hat." More angry than anxious, Caroline was having none of it. She elbowed him in the stomach and caught him off-balance. Malcolm Pearson added impetus by squeezing in beside Caroline and shoving her along until the intruder was forced out of the door and into the road. As they drove off, their would-be travelling companion scurried into another cab directly behind them, which promptly set off in hot pursuit.

They had been well briefed by insiders, before they went, on the different techniques the KBG would use to follow them. First was the high-profile approach: you were supposed to be aware that an agent was following you and therefore be intimidated by him. The second option was a more subtle surveillance, designed to leave you guessing. Most troublesome was the third option: the discreet spy you would never know about. The man in the fur hat fell squarely into the first category.

Caroline had two items on her agenda: to get to a phone, and to find a worshipping church. They broke this news to the cab driver as gently as possible. Firstly they asked him about the church. Then Malcolm casually said he could do with having a word with his business back in Europe, and would the driver mind taking them to a telephone? The taxi driver became extremely guarded and uneasy. "It was as if every word we were saying could be heard in the car behind," Malcolm said later. The driver fell silent. Malcolm and Caroline exchanged looks and changed the subject. A backward glance through the rear window confirmed that the man in the fur hat was still on their tail.

They had been driving for about ten minutes when the Volga swerved to the right without warning, and the taxi driver said, very loudly, "I've decided not to take you to the church I originally intended; instead I'm going to take you to another church." He veered off down a side street, losing the cab behind them. The cabby waited till it was out of view, then cautiously pointed across the road.

There was a church, and opposite that, a telephone. Later, back at the hotel, Caroline and Malcolm conspicuously made their arrangements for the press conference. Using the hotel phone, they called several well-known dissidents. *The Times'* Moscow bureau was put in the picture. It was as if they had made an announcement to the KGB: we know that you know, but break this up and you'll have a diplomatic incident on your hands.

Playing for keeps

Valery Senderov knew they were coming. Since his release from the gulag, the mathematician had been relegated to working as a night porter in a factory. Cox and Pearson arranged to hold the press conference in his apartment the following day. Among the invited guests were representatives of the independent journal, *Glasnost*, and the *Ekspress Khronika*, one of the main "samizdat" (clandestine) newspapers.

The theme of the press conference was "Democracy and the Rule of Law". Twenty people crowded into the small apartment room, which had been stripped of furniture except for a huddle of chairs and a table strewn with copies of the *Ekspress Khronika*. The delegates knew very well that they were being bugged by the KGB, yet were determined to talk openly about their hopes for a free, democratic Russia. In fact, Senderov's telephone had been cut off by the KGB. Policies were discussed for reform and for transforming agriculture and the economy. Before the meeting ended, the participants had given the KGB plenty to think about.

"It was very subversive," Caroline reflected years later. "The dissidents were playing a high-risk game." All of them knew the risks and were prepared to be sent back to the gulags. But they were worried that younger and lesser-known dissidents were being targeted, and if the high-profile names were silenced, there would be nobody to speak for the next generation of activists. Having a British parliamentarian in their midst ensured a level of publicity that would make the KGB think twice about sending any of them back to the gulag.

Caroline and Malcolm's flight from Moscow was booked for the following day. To celebrate a successful conference, they planned to take Valery Senderov out for a meal. At the first two hotels, the moment the doorman caught sight of Senderov, he slammed the door in his face. At the third restaurant, Caroline insisted on walking in first. As the doorman made way for the wealthy-looking Western woman, she ushered in Valery, with Malcolm following on behind.

As they ate, Senderov talked about his time in the gulags, where he had spent a considerable period in solitary confinement. He was still pale and almost skeletal-looking. He told them it had been so cold in the winter that a veneer of ice had formed on the inside of his cell. When their ration of food was distributed on alternate days, it consisted of cold water and mouldy bread. He used to keep his sanity by working out advanced and complex mathematical equations. Yet Senderov thanked God for the period in the prison camps, because, in his words, "It made me a better Christian."

"Can you explain what you mean?" Caroline urged.

"I mean that through all that suffering, although I hated the system that put me there and kept me there, I praise God that I never, ever, hated my jailers."

Senderov believed that the soil of Russian consciousness was fertile and he spoke optimistically about the future. Spirituality had survived the dark years like a mushroom spore. Senderov explained that when the light was able to shine again, Russia's spirit would respond and grow. Religion had not been stamped out by seventy years of communism, but was alive, although quiescent, and would flourish again. "He kept this incredible tranquility and equanimity," recalls Caroline. "His face was almost translucent with spirituality. I have a huge respect and admiration for him."

During that brutally cold visit ubiquitous injustices, both large and small, seemed to chill the atmosphere even more. Certainly the warmth of Russian hospitality and the opportunity to help the dissidents by smuggling their samizdat documents into the West made all the risks worthwhile. And just as she had seen abuses on a small scale at the Polytechnic of North London, here Caroline Cox saw the massive abuse of a nation, and its inevitable deprivations, loss of freedom, and absence of hope.

It wasn't long before she learned that – again – it was the children who paid the highest price for living in those unforgiving surroundings. Especially hopeless were the orphans. And most hopeless of all were the orphans who had been declared, by the state, to be "oligophrenic". "Oligophrenic" means, in simple terms, "little-brained" or feeble-minded. However, the director of Kashchenko Psychiatric Hospital in Moscow, Vladimir Kozyrev, offered a different explanation. "In Russia," he explained, "to become orphaned or abandoned is virtually synonymous with becoming an oligophrenic."

Although she had read about the oligophrenic boys and girls and their plight, Baroness Cox had not seen these particular children's circumstances for herself until 1990, when she visited a children's orphanage for oligophrenics in Leningrad (which reverted to its old name of St Petersburg in 1991). She later described them as "well-dressed, bright, lively and eager to talk. Yet they were described to their faces as oligophrenic and totally incapable of ever doing a normal job or living a normal life."

Caroline's first surprise was to find that these "little-brained" children were able to compete with her at table tennis. They looked, spoke, and moved like ordinary kids. A few were even playing chess. Not only were they doomed to a facility that categorised them as mentally unfit for normal society, but they also faced a future that made no room for them because of their so-called disabilities. There would be no trade school for them, no college, not even routine jobs. The children's categorisation prevented them from anything more productive than being cannon fodder for the Soviet factory system, prostitution, alcoholism, or serving in the Red Army, where many of the young boys were trained from pre-adolescence to be ruthless killers.

The next morning Caroline Cox was invited to Leningrad's psychiatric hospital to witness the fate of those who ran away from the orphanages. She entered a nightmare, a hellish environment for the children confined there. The boys and girls were locked in filthy wards with urine-soaked mattresses. Their minds were ravaged by the same drugs that were used to torture Soviet dissidents, drugs such as Sulfozin, which caused cramps and high fever. To this day she has not forgotten a little boy named Igor, with his white pinched face and a shock of dirty brown hair, coming to her in tears and pleading, "Please will you find me a mother? I want to get out of here."

She went out into the courtyard and wept.

Haunted by all she had seen and heard, Caroline Cox returned to Russia in the autumn of 1991, with a team of child development professionals including clinical and educational psychologists and a paediatrician. Their assessments of 171 children affirmed that around two-thirds of the orphans were average or above average in intelligence. Nonetheless, those boys and girls would bear the stigma of mental incapacity for the rest of their lives.

In *Crisis Magazine* (1 February 2004), Benedict Rogers – a good friend and colleague of Caroline Cox – wrote of that journey's results in his article "The Unconventional Baroness":

> In the dying days of the Soviet Union, she visited
> state-run orphanages in Leningrad and was

horrified. There she found "bright, able, articulate
children" misdiagnosed as "oligophrenics" or
mentally handicapped. She wrote a report,
"Trajectories of Despair", that sent shockwaves
through the Russian system. Her damning
conclusions could have ensured her a lifetime ban
from visiting Russia again, but instead the Russians
turned to her for help.

She was invited to the Kremlin by the Russian Federation's
Minister of Education, who thanked her for her report and then
asked a startling question: "Lady Cox, will you help us change the
whole childcare system for the whole of Russia?" This minister
wanted to transform the existing system from orphanages to
foster-family residences, which had not been known in Russia
for the seventy years of Soviet Communism.

Caroline Cox signed the contract with what she described
as terror and elation – terror, because she had no money and
no professional resources; elation, because here was a break-
through, an opportunity to make a real difference in many young
lives. Then came another request: Moscow's city government
proposed, "If we give you the building, will you establish the first
foster family here in Moscow to serve as a model for the rest of
the nation?" Caroline signed that contract with the same mixed
emotions. "Again," she said later, "I had no resources. But what
an opportunity!"

By 1994 Baroness Cox, in conjunction with dedicated Russian
colleagues, had established the new programme for orphans,
called "Our Family", which began caring for orphaned children
in family environments. And its eventual goal had already been
established – to set up a system of foster care throughout Russia
which would provide a transitional residence for boys and girls,

many of them declared "oligophrenic". Without fostering, these lost boys and girls would often go directly from orphanages onto the streets, and often found their way too quickly into prostitution, organised crime, drugs, and alcohol.

Our Family also began to work on a second objective: to develop proposals for amendments and changes in Russian legislation in favour of foster care. Directed by Maria Ternovskaya, the organisation cared for hundreds of children. Since the beginning, Ternovskaya and her colleagues have trained representatives from forty-six Russian regions (about 5,000 professionals in total). Twenty-nine regions developed similar projects, and seventeen regions approved regional legislation in support of foster care and professional services.

In January 2007 Our Family was launched as an indigenous and independent Russian organisation. The famous pianist and second son of Aleksandr Solzhenitsyn, Ignat, gave a performance in Moscow attended by His Royal Highness Prince Michael of Kent, the evening's guest of honour. This event celebrated the coming of age of Our Family and its transition into a fully fledged Russian charitable organisation, independent of Western funding.

Karabakh: Armenia's battleground

Russia was not the only former Soviet Socialist Republic to be faced with exceptional turmoil. Once the imploding USSR had collapsed, chaos ensued in many of its former satellites. And in the small, ancient country of Armenia – more specifically in Nagorno-Karabakh, a tiny Christian enclave comprised predominately of Armenians and relocated by Stalin in Azerbaijan – an unjust and violent scenario began to unfold almost immediately after the demise of the Iron Curtain. By1990 violence was escalating and would soon once again devastate a long-suffering people, already scarred by centuries of violence, including the Turkish massacres of the late nineteenth century and culminating in the genocide of 1.5 million Armenians in the early twentieth century. Another part of the tragic story was the annexation of Western Armenia, now known as Eastern Turkey. This region includes Mount Ararat, Armenia's national symbol, which still remains captive behind the Turkish border.

Baroness Cox, when invited to a conference organised by Yelena Bonner, the widow of the Russian dissident Andrei Sakharov, first visited Nagorno-Karabakh in 1989. In Sakharov's view, "For Azerbaijan the issue of Karabakh is a matter of ambition. For the Armenians of Karabakh, it is a matter of life and death." Like an enormous Goliath bearing down on a small and pitifully armed David, Azerbaijan began a policy of ethnic cleansing of the Armenians of Nagorno-Karabakh.

Once again, a faithful Christian community faced injustice and grave loss. Once again, the weakest and most vulnerable citizens, the children, paid the most heartbreaking price. And, once again, the need for aid and international advocacy was immediate and desperate. But this was a raging battle, not a cold war. Machine guns ripped human bodies apart, shells decimated houses, and rockets demolished villages, churches, and monasteries. Besides the mounting death toll, a horrific detritus of deforming and disabling injuries followed in the wake of the violence.

For Caroline Cox, as a frontline witness to this war and a lonely voice raised in defence of a just cause, the impact of Nagorno-Karabakh's agony was more profound than she could possibly have imagined. The battle itself, which had begun in a Stalinist context, became transformed into one that included

Afghan-trained mujahedin warriors. The Karabakh conflict was not a religious war. But as Azerbaijan, despite its military superiority, began to lose, it drew on its Islamic contacts to recruit the mujahedin as mercenaries. Nothing could more clearly highlight Armenia's vulnerability, lying not only on a geological fault line, but also on geopolitical and spiritual fault lines, where East meets West, and Christianity meets Islam.

Chapter Three

Nagorno-Karabakh –
Dignity is a Crown of Thorns

Behind the church podium she stands poised and alert, neatly dressed in a burgundy suit and white blouse, her brown coif gleaming in the dim light. As she speaks about the countries where HART (Humanitarian Aid Relief Trust), the aid and advocacy organisation Baroness Cox founded) is working, the scene on the projection screen behind her changes from a jungle in South East Asia to a group of serious-looking Armenian men positioned near a helicopter, the wind from its rotors tousling their hair. Her presentation has moved to another locale that is dear to her heart, whose people have been subjected to heart-rending suffering.

"And finally," she says, "come with me to the mountains of Nagorno-Karabakh – a small part of ancient Armenia cut off by Stalin in the 1920s and relocated as a little enclave in Azerbaijan."

She continues:

> *The Armenians have suffered greatly throughout*
> *history, being the victims of the first genocide of*

*the last century, when 1.5 million Armenians were
slaughtered, and all of Western Armenia annexed,
by Turkey. Then, in the 1920s, Stalin cut off part of
Eastern Armenia, Nagorno-Karabakh, and located
it as a separate region within Azerbaijan. With the
dissolution of the Soviet Union in the late 1980s,
Azerbaijan began to undertake ethnic cleansing of
the 150,000 Armenians living in this little enclave
and they tried to defend themselves against
impossible odds.*

She concludes her presentation as the weary face of an old man
appears on the screen behind her.

*Finally, may I introduce a farmer from Karabakh:
at the beginning of the process of attempted ethnic
cleansing from 1990–94, Azerbaijan undertook a
series of deportations of entire villages. They were
brutal operations, in which innocent villagers were
rounded up, many were maltreated, some murdered;
homes were ransacked; then the people were forcibly
driven off their land, unable to take anything with
them.*

*During one of these terrible events, at Getashen,
a farmer managed to escape into the mountains.
Devastated by what he had just witnessed, he saw
an apricot tree in blossom and went to it for comfort,
as it was so beautiful. Then, to his horror, he saw
hanging from a branch the body of a five-year old
Armenian girl, cut in two. He wept and vowed revenge.*

*When we met him two years later, he wept again,
telling us that he felt very bad, as he had broken*

his vow; for when the Armenians captured an Azeri
village, he could not bring himself to harm a child.

An American colleague stood up, removed his
baseball cap and said: "Thank you. For the first
time in my life, I understand what the Bible means
when it says, "vengeance is mine, I will repay", saith
the Lord'. And thank you for the dignity you have
shown."

To this, the farmer replied in words I will never
forget: "Dignity," he quietly replied, "is a crown of
thorns."

The cauldron of the Caucasus

In recent years, that crown of thorns has been worn by increasing numbers of Christians in some of the world's most notorious sites of suffering and persecution. However, until recently, few people in the West had heard of Nagorno-Karabakh, a mountainous scrap of Transcaucasia tucked inside Azerbaijan. Karabakh has long survived as a fragment of Armenia, isolated but for a highway that long connected it, however tenuously, to its motherland. It is a beautiful, mountainous region rich in pastureland, sparkling with clear rivers and streams. Straddling the borders of Turkey and Armenia is Mount Ararat, where biblical tradition says that Noah's ark came to rest.

However, despite being a crossroads of the world, Armenia has suffered more than its fair share during epochs of war-torn history, none bloodier than the twentieth century. Much of this is due to its proximity to Turkey. According to historian C. W. Hostler in *Turkism and the Soviets* (London, 1957), on the eve of World War I, Nazim Bey – Turkey's Minister of War – declared,

"Our state must be purely Turkish...we must Turkify non-Turkish nationalities by force."

That idea of Turkish "purity" resulted in the genocide which erupted in 1915, when a political group called the Young Turks launched a programme to systematically rid Turkey of all Armenians. It was carried out with a savagery that served as a prototype for the Holocaust, which Adolf Hitler himself noted. Armenians were burned alive, hanged, and even crucified. Multiple thousands of men were murdered while hundreds of thousands of women, elders, and children were sent on death marches across the desert. When it was over, three-quarters of Turkey's 2 million Armenians had been slaughtered.

During World War I, Armenia became a battleground for conflicts between Turkey and Russia. When the revolution at home recalled Russia from the war effort in 1917, Turkish troops began rolling across Armenia and Azerbaijan. Christian Armenians in Baku, the capital of Azerbaijan, battled against the approaching Muslim Azeri-Turks. In 1920, violence broke out between Armenians and Azeris in the town of Shusha (also known as Shushi in Armenian). Of the 45,000 killed, two-thirds were Armenian.

Not long afterwards, Azerbaijan, Karabakh, and much of Armenia were swallowed up in the emergent Soviet Union – the USSR. Resorting to the ancient strategy of divide-and-rule, in 1921 Joseph Stalin declared that Nagorno-Karabakh belonged not to Armenia but to Azerbaijan, along with the four-mile Lachin corridor, which had been its lifeline to Armenia. The Azeri response was also an ancient one: launch a population exchange.

In subsequent years, the Soviets shifted Armenians to Azerbaijan, where they would be in a minority, and moved Azeri settlers into Karabakh. To enforce cultural assimilation,

Karabakh's Armenian churches, newspapers, and schools were closed down. Armenians seeking higher education were required to study outside the enclave. To make matters worse, they were not permitted to take up employment in the homeland, including those who were educationally qualified.

During glasnost, in February 1988, the Supreme Soviet of Nagorno-Karabakh called for the transfer of their enclave from Azerbaijan to Armenia. By July they had voted to secede. Demonstrations in favour of unification took place in Karabakh and Armenia, and in a counter-demonstration two Azeris were killed in Stepanakert – the capital of Nagorno-Karabakh. In response, a wave of anti-Armenian violence broke out in Azerbaijan.

Armenians were massacred in the industrial town of Sumgait. Before long, the tide of Armenian refugees fleeing from Azerbaijan rose to what a 1995 Council of Europe Report estimated to be around 350,000. In the USA, Andrei Sakharov warned, "The Armenian people are again facing the threat of genocide."

Then came a massive earthquake. In December 1988, an enormous seismic upheaval devastated the region, claimed between 25,000 and 50,000 lives and rendered up to half a million homeless. The epicentre of the quake hit a resettlement area for Armenian refugees, and the disaster was celebrated on the streets of Azerbaijan. And within eighteen months, virtually all the Azeri-Turks in Armenia had been deported or fled, amounting to some 185,000 people.

Meanwhile, there were continuous deportations in Karabakh and Azerbaijan, until almost all the 400,000 ethnic Armenians had fled or were forced to leave. Those who went to Armenia numbered 330,000; others escaped to Russia, with only a few remaining in Azerbaijan. There were meetings. There were negotiations. There were vague and unspecified pledges and continuous threats. Ultimately, the USSR rejected the transfer of Karabakh to Armenia and the decision ignited a firestorm.

In 1990 Nagorno-Karabakh – which is sometimes known by its ancient name of Artsakh – had set up its own rival national council and now witnessed its members rounded up and arrested. Viktor Polianitchku, a KGB officer and second secretary of the Azerbaijani Communist Party, had silenced the press and arrested the Armenian leadership. Within a month, Soviet Interior Ministry troops, backed by Azeri special forces – the OMON black berets – launched an attack against Armenian villages to the north of Karabakh. Villagers were given an ultimatum to leave, so their homes could be turned over to Azeri refugees.

Then, in spring 1991, came Operation Ring – a military noose meant to strangle Karabakh and achieve the depopulation of Armenians from their villages and towns. It demanded the systematic deportation of Armenians from the enclave's villages, carried out by the combined 23rd Division of the Soviet Fourth Army and forces of the Azerbaijani Ministry of the Interior, the OMON.

When the Azeri troops moved in, Galia Saoukhanin, a 29-year-old mother from the village of Nakhichevanik, was forced to flee with her two small children. She revealed her horrendous experience:

> They killed the population here: all who couldn't escape; the elderly people who couldn't run. My brother was killed. My brother-in-law was killed. It changed my destiny and my soul. For months my children were crying without stopping. I have a terrible fear inside me. I dream every night how I

am going to escape and where I am going to keep
my children.

No one could have been prepared for the savagery of the
Azeri onslaught. Medical worker Movses Poghossian followed
behind the conflict, picking up the human remains of atrocity
after atrocity. "There are bodies without eyes, without ears...
they are cutting crosses, they cut off hands."

It was against this backdrop of violence that Baroness Cox
was introduced to the tragedy of Nagorno-Karabakh. She later
described that first encounter, in May 1991.

> *I had been asked to lead a delegation of human*
> *rights experts from the Andrei Sakharov Memorial*
> *Congress in Moscow to obtain evidence of the*
> *violations of human rights inflicted on the*
> *Armenians of Artsakh during Azerbaijan's brutal*
> *policy of "Operation Ring".*
>
> *Having heard the evidence of the suffering of the*
> *Armenians deported from places such as Getashen,*
> *Martunashen and Berdadzor, I and my colleagues*
> *decided that we needed to hear the Azeri version of*
> *events. However, the Azeris refused us permission to*
> *fly to Stepanakert, so we agreed amongst ourselves to*
> *do the next best thing: to walk across the border with*
> *a white flag.*
>
> *We flew by helicopter to Voskepar, where we left*
> *the friendly pilots to undertake the crazy mission of*
> *walking into Azerbaijan, where we were met by very*
> *hostile OMON and regular army commanders who*
> *were not very pleased by our unorthodox approach.*
>
> *However, it was essential to hear both the*

*Armenian and Azeri points of view. As human
rights activists, we try to follow the example of
Andrei Sakharov who always worked on the side
of the victim. We therefore had to find the evidence
to show who are the primary aggressors and who
are the victims of aggression. Our visit to Voskepar
provided this evidence and made it possible for us
to begin our advocacy on behalf of the Armenian
people and especially of those suffering in the war
for Artsakh.*

*When we returned to Britain, we were able to
give an interview with the BBC, who said they would
not have broadcasted our report if we had not heard
the Azeri as well as the Armenian views.*

Running drugs in a war zone

Baroness Cox visited Nagorno-Karabakh repeatedly during
the early 1990s war. As the fighting ground on, one of the most
troubling elements for her was the lack of medical supplies for
the wounded. During a visit to Stepanakert's hard-hit hospital in
January 1991, she confirmed for herself horror stories she'd heard
of surgical operations without anaesthetics, deadly infections
without antibiotics, primitive conditions without electricity or
running water. She witnessed the pitiful conditions endured by
the patients. As she was a nurse, these matters were particularly
disturbing for her, since she was fully aware of what could and
should have been available to Armenian medics.

Before she left the country, Karabakh's military authorities
gave Caroline Cox a list of their most urgent priorities, including
hard drugs such as morphine, and cocaine powder for eye

injuries. Once she was back in England, she made calls to anyone and everyone who might help with funding, procurement, and transport. Before long she became, in her own words, "an international drugs carrier".

The Home Office gave her a license to purchase and export the restricted drugs. In January 1992, the medications were packed into two substantial plywood crates, marked "Fragile, Handle with Care", and Caroline Cox was faced with the challenge of transporting them to Armenia. After a rather unorthodox journey on a Soviet cargo plane, Cox, her travelling companions, and the medications arrived in Yerevan on a cold, crisp day, where they were transferred to a military helicopter that would take them to Stepanakert. Joining them was a medical team and a worried-looking Zori Balayan, the elected representative for Karabakh on the Supreme Soviet of the USSR, as well as a physician and the distinguished author of more than fifty books. He reported that the Azeris had escalated the conflict significantly in recent days with the use of Grad (BM-21) missiles.

Grads had been used to devastating effect in Afghanistan and were banned by international convention. They were fired in multiples of forty. If they exploded outside a building they did major damage to the exterior. If they penetrated the building's wall, the entire structure was shattered from within by a whirlwind of shrapnel. In Shaumyan, to the north of Karabakh, two schools had been pulverised. Because of the devastating injuries the Grads had caused, the Cox party made a stop in Shaumyan to offload some morphine and other painkilling drugs.

As the helicopter took off again on its way to Stepanakert, the cloud cover was so thick and visibility so poor that the pilot soon announced they could not continue; they would have to sit out the bad weather on the ground. He located a break in the clouds and landed at Horator.

And Caroline and her colleagues found themselves stranded in Azeri-held territory.

The only way out was to walk. She and the others were all too aware of the dangers of exposure – both to the frigid weather and to snipers. After many hours' walking through the forest and thick snow, they found their way to a local village, which, providentially, was Armenian. The villagers invited them into their homes to eat, drink, and thaw out around log fires. A stone was later set up to commemorate the walk, which the locals called "Cox Way".

The following day, the group completed its journey to Stepanakert. Just twelve days had passed since Caroline Cox's last visit to the hospital. She was saddened to find that conditions were even worse than before because the facility had come under heavy fire. Alazan rockets and artillery shells had struck even as surgeons were performing an operation. The separate maternity hospital had also taken a direct hit. Mothers and babies had been transferred to the basement, where they were still being cared for in freezing, damp conditions that invited hypothermia. A number of mothers had given birth prematurely. The drugs and medical supplies were immediately distributed by the hospital's grateful staff. From that day on, no further deaths were reported from pain-induced shock during surgery without anaesthetic.

It would be four more months before the Red Cross was able to follow in Baroness Cox's footsteps and enter Karabakh. She later described the mission:

During 1991, I visited Azerbaijan in July, to obtain a fuller version of Azerbaijan's policies; I then travelled to Armenia and Karabakh in October. In December, full-scale war broke out. I was appalled by the situation. There was constant bombardment

> *of Stepanakert from Shushi. Electricity had been*
> *cut off by Azerbaijan, so women and children were*
> *trapped in basements and cellars, with no light, heat*
> *or running water.*
>
> *In the hospital, casualties of war were suffering*
> *horrific injuries. But with Artsakh besieged,*
> *blockaded and bombarded, the Armenian doctors*
> *had virtually no medicines, including no painkillers*
> *or anaesthetics. I could not sleep when I returned*
> *to Britain, thinking of that unrelieved pain, so we*
> *managed to obtain a large consignment of medicines*
> *and returned twelve days later.*

In May 1992, Armenia and Azerbaijan inked their signatures on a peace agreement in Tehran. The following day, another Azeri offensive began. All attempts to mediate in the conflict had failed. Armenia's plea to the UN to send in peacekeepers fell on deaf ears. On 1 September 1992, *The New York Times* warned: "Without political intervention, the deadly little war will degenerate to the levels of Bosnia." In fact, it already had.

The battle for Shushi

Around 400 Grad missiles a day were launched from the heights of Shushi, bombarding the civilian population in Stepanakert below. It was imperative to stop the missiles. But there was another compelling reason for Karabakh to reclaim Shushi – the town straddled the main road connecting Nagorno-Karabakh to Armenia. Shushi's fall would enable food and arms to go through unchecked. It might even turn the tide of the war.

The battle for Shushi was, however, a military strategist's

nightmare, for two reasons. The assault on the fortress town would put at risk a significant portion of Karabakh's already depleted forces. And, as a treasured historic centre of Armenian culture, Shushi had to remain as undamaged by further conflict as possible.

Karabakh's strategists devised a ruse – they persuaded the Azeris that they were being attacked by an enormous force by driving their few vehicles round and round at night, revving their engines and making as much noise and clamour as they could muster. A corridor was left open for Azeri soldiers and remaining civilians to escape. As hoped, they fled en masse, resulting in fewer casualties on both sides than had been feared. The official figure for Armenian losses was thirty-two dead and thirty-six wounded.

The fall of Shushi was a military triumph. From Caroline Cox's perspective, the whole conflict had acquired a biblical dimension. "It was like Gideon driving out the Midianites: the odds were impossible. The whole of Karabakh had a remaining population of some 140,000, including women and children. They were fighting against more than 7 million Azeris, assisted by battle-hardened mercenaries. And yet they prevailed."

But that wasn't the end of it – then, or later.

There were disturbing reports about radical Islamist forces. Azerbaijan had recruited up to 3,000 mercenaries, including mujahedin veterans of the Afghan conflict, jihadists who were eager for fresh opportunities to drive back the infidel. And if the prospect of a jihad was insufficiently enticing, there was also the promise of large amounts of money – enough money to create a long line of volunteers outside the Iranian consulate in Pakistan. And, according to State Defence Minister Vazguen Sarkissian, in a 1994 interview with author Andrew Boyd, Saudi Arabian funds had reportedly been invested in the recruitment drive.

The reality of a Muslim vs Christian dimension to the war was understandably played down within Karabakh. "It is not a religious war," said Bishop Martirosian on more than one occasion. "But there is a danger with the Azeris using *mujahedin* that they may internationalise the conflict and make it a religious war." And, in contrast to Azerbaijan's well-documented policy of destroying Christian holy places, an Armenian team of restorers was dispatched into Shushi to repair whatever damage the war had inflicted on the local mosque.

In April 1992, Azerbaijani troops attacked the town of Maraghar, leaving behind evidence of unspeakable cruelty. More than 100 women and children had been kidnapped, most of the town was looted then burned to the ground, and forty-five villagers had been beheaded – their heads sawn off and their bodies burned. Caroline Cox visited the remains of the town the next day when homes were still smouldering and interviewed survivors, recognising that the massacre was but one of many such brutal attacks by the Azeris. A traumatised mother told her:

> They attacked the village and started cutting the
> villagers to pieces. I myself heard the screams
> of a man who was having his head cut off by a
> saw. Then we took our children and ran away.
> The next day we returned to the village. People
> were cut into pieces, their eyes were gouged out,
> their ears were cut off. We then saw the [body
> of the] man whom I had previously seen being
> decapitated. The saw was lying next to him and
> all the blood had flowed out of the body. Another
> man – our uncle – was tied to the back of a tank
> and was dragged 500 metres. After that we fled

> to Shaumyan. Ten days later, the Azeri-Turks did
> the same things. After that I took the children
> and fled. We walked for 40 miles. We arrived
> thirsty and hungry and with our clothes in tatters.
> We couldn't take anything with us. I've seen these
> atrocities with my own eyes.

After leaving the village of Maraghar, Caroline Cox visited the hospital in the regional capital town of Mardakert. There she met the head nurse who had just fled from the village. Fourteen of her relatives had been slaughtered, and she had seen her own son's head sawn off. As Caroline embraced her they wept together. After the traumatised nurse had finished sobbing, Caroline said to her, "Would you find it comforting to give a message to the world? To tell them what has happened to your people?" Caroline watched in wonder as the woman's countenance changed, her expression transformed from grief to dignity. She replied,

> Like you, I'm a nurse and I have worked in this
> hospital for a long time. I have seen how the
> medicines you brought saved many lives and
> eased so much pain. I therefore just want to say
> thank you. Thank you to all those people who
> have not forgotten us in these terrible days.

The days were, indeed, terrible. Forty per cent of Karabakh was overrun and Azeri troops were within ten miles of Stepanakert. Longer-range missiles were being used, launched from locations beyond the reach of Karabakh defence forces. The civilian casualty rate soared. The enclave was rapidly becoming depopulated. Almost all the Azeri-Turk civilians had left or been driven from their homes. Now, Nagorno-Karabakh's remaining able-bodied citizens were making the hazardous journey to a safe haven in Armenia.

In August 1992, the Azeris pressed aircraft into the conflict. SU25s started dropping 500-kilogramme bombs on Stepanakert and the surrounding villages. By October, cluster bombs were deployed, which are banned for use against civilians under international law. Also banned was the use of flechettes, dart-like bullets with fins designed to maximise damage to human tissue. Surgeons were soon struggling to remove flechettes from soldiers coming in from the battlefield. But the cluster bombs were far less discriminating. The attractive-looking silver balls, primed to explode when touched, attracted children like magnets.

Twelve-year-old Pailak Haratunian was playing in the woods with his friends when he picked up one of the silver balls and decided to carry it home. He fell. The explosion tore out one eye, damaged the other, injured his leg and chest, and perforated his colon. Maria Bedelian, also twelve, found a ball in her garden in a village near Stepanakert. As she was taking it to show her mother, she tripped. Seven people were wounded in the explosion. Maria's left leg was splintered like a twig and she suffered multiple injuries. The surgeons didn't know where to start. A weary doctor in Stepanakert shook his head in disbelief. "This is not the front line," he protested. "These are *children*."

When Caroline Cox heard reports of these injuries, she visited the children in the hospital. Sickened by what she saw and heard, she gathered her evidence and documented her findings in the seminal report: "Ethnic Cleansing in Progress: War in Nagorno-Karabakh", co-authored by Dr John Eibner. The more she learned about the people's suffering, the more determined she was that the British government should condemn the atrocities.

Ashamed to be British

Armed with photos and interviews, the Baroness arranged a meeting at the Foreign Office with a senior politician. She pointed out that Azerbaijan was a signatory to the major conventions on human rights and a member of the Conference on Security and Co-operation in Europe (CSCE). "Therefore, would the British government prevail upon Azerbaijan," she queried, "to stop dropping cluster bombs on children, which is a gross violation of human rights?"

The senior politician, who must remain unnamed, coolly replied, "No country has an interest in other countries, only interests. And we have oil interests in Azerbaijan. Good morning." And he showed her to the door.

"I went back home and wept," she said later, describing her sense of powerlessness and dismay when a government, which might have done something to save the lives of innocent civilians, put oil interests first.

In the days that followed she visited British Petroleum (BP), requesting guarantees that oil profits would not be invested in weapons; that a share of the profits would be distributed among the victims of war, both Armenian and Azeri, and for BP to exert its influence to prevent Azerbaijan from imposing a military solution. British Petroleum declined all her requests. And as for Britain's Foreign Office policy, as far as Baroness Cox was concerned, there was no way that was going to remain behind closed doors.

She rose to her feet in the House of Lords and looked across the elegantly decorated chamber. It was a setting that would appeal to the pride of any British patriot. But on that occasion, she felt no surge of satisfaction. Before all the assembled peers, she reported her conversation with the Foreign Office official.

She later concluded:

> *For the first time in my life, I felt ashamed to be*
> *British. I can understand strategic interests. I can*
> *understand commercial interests, but I didn't think*
> *it is the long-term interest of any country to let*
> *those obliterate concern for human rights. Moreover,*
> *I didn't think the majority of British people would*
> *actually want oil at the price of cluster bombs*
> *on children.*

New century, new turmoil and tragedy

Caroline Cox's eyes still light up when she speaks of the people she has come to love in Nagorno-Karabakh – courageous men and women who have worked as hard to rebuild their land as to defend it – including the inspirational staff of the Lady Cox Rehabilitation Centre in Stepanakert, founded in 1998 and directed to this day by the indefatigable Vardan Tadevosyan. The health facility has become an internationally recognised "Centre of Excellence", providing hope and healing to over 1,500 patients every year, while helping to break the stigma of disability prevalent throughout the former Soviet Union.

Caroline cherishes her special bond with the Centre's patients and staff, as well her friendship with Karabakh's military heroes, elected officials, church leaders, medical workers, and citizens who, like the old farmer, know that dignity can be a crown of thorns. And the people return her love. She is, in their eyes, a living saint, or, as one woman put it, "our Mother Teresa". But, from then until now, Baroness Cox has remained deeply concerned about Artsakh's future.

And, confirming her worst fears, in September 2020 violence erupted once again. For forty-four days, the people of Nagorno-Karabakh endured almost daily military offensives by tanks, drones, helicopters, cluster bombs, and Smerch multiple rocket launchers – weapons incapable of precision targeting – in breach of international humanitarian law and Geneva conventions. The precise death toll is unknown but an estimated 14,000 civilian structures were damaged or destroyed, including homes, schools, religious sites, markets, and infrastructure vital to the survival of the local population, such as bridges, electricity, telecoms, gas, and water supply systems. Heavy shelling caused mass displacement: early estimates suggest that as many as 100,000 civilians were forced to flee, although many remained, taking shelter in churches and basements. Those who have since made the difficult decision to return face a monumental task in rebuilding their cities and towns.

It is within this context that Baroness Cox, accompanied by Revd David Thomas, arrived in Nagorno-Karabakh for her eighty-ninth visit since the early 1990s. They saw hundreds of vehicles loaded with personal possessions and firewood from trees, fleeing on congested roads from their homeland now occupied by Azerbaijani forces. Some families had set fire to their homes so they would not be available for occupation, while local farmers herded their cattle and sheep towards Armenia.

Due to the Covid-19 pandemic that was dangerously surging across the globe at the time, Caroline and David were repeatedly warned by health authorities for their sake to wear masks at all times, not to embrace the refugees they would encounter, to continue to sanitise their hands, and to maintain appropriate "social distance" from them. However, as Caroline explained later, "that was impossible". As she found herself among shattered, grieving refugees, she could do nothing less than open her arms to them, weep with them, encourage them, and hold them close to her heart. And, thankfully, she later reported that she had remained uninfected by coronavirus.

Despite the chaos of war and a raging pandemic, the irresistible gratitude of the Armenians shone through. During a poignant visit to Dadivank Monastery – on the penultimate day before the area was handed over to Azerbaijan – David spoke to three sisters who requested a photo with him.

> They asked us if we were smiling for the photo.
> "No," David replied.
> "Then we must take it again!" one of the sisters
> said. "This is God's place," she explained. "And we
> must be happy here."

Of course, remaining happy wasn't a natural response. Caroline learned that this time, during this devastating conflict, beautiful Shushi had not been spared. On 8 October 2020, the town's Ghazanchetsots Cathedral, beautifully restored after the desecration and damage inflicted during the previous war, was shelled twice by Azeri forces and badly damaged. The town was later occupied by Azeri forces, who claimed to have "restored an ancient Azeri town to the Azeri people". Clearly this view is widely disputed, given the community's complex history.

Equally poignant was a visit to refugees from Karabakh who were sheltering in church buildings in the town of Saghmosavan, near Yerevan, Armenia's capital. They described their intense suffering caused by the loss of loved ones, as well as their inability to find out about the whereabouts or survival of friends and family members. This accompanied feelings of despair over the prospect of destitution; most refugees and displaced persons have no idea how they are going to survive and care for their families.

Meanwhile, Armine Aleksanyan, Deputy Foreign Minister of Nagorno-Karabakh, wasted no words describing present realities in a meeting with Baroness Cox and Revd Thomas:

> Azerbaijan violated multiple ceasefires within minutes. They used weapons forbidden by international law against civilians. 46 kindergartens and 53 schools were damaged. Foreign terrorists, recruited and deployed by Turkey, beheaded civilians. Even today, subversive groups are entering our villages and towns. One grandma was captured and beheaded.
>
> The world watched and did nothing. International organisations did nothing to prevent the suffering of civilians. They responded with indifference and inaction. Shame on everyone who watched daily killings of civilians and did nothing to help in any tangible way. Action was needed but nothing was done. Even with all the reports in the international media, the world did nothing to protect the value of human life. Azerbaijan and Turkey now know they can continue crimes against humanity with impunity.
>
> An estimated 150,000 people were targets of Azerbaijan and Turkey, with significant political and military help. [Regarding the 1915-23 Armenian Genocide] President Erdogan declared that it was time to complete what was unfinished 100 years ago.

Caroline recalled during one of the more painful conversations with refugees, "As we wept together," she said, "a twelve-year old boy sat down at a piano and began to play beautiful music. We were so profoundly moved by his talent and by the community's commitment to maintain their precious culture even in the midst such overwhelming losses."

The cultural beauty has indeed survived. But the stories are horrifying. Knar Avanisyan Varangatag was thirty years old:

> My husband, a firefighter, was killed on 30
> September during Azeri attacks in the North, in
> the Mataghis region of Martakert. His body was
> so destroyed that we needed DNA to identify
> him. I don't know what to say to my four children.
> They asked me this morning about him, and why
> he has stopped sending money. What can I say?
>
> We hid under trees to escape the UAVs
> and aerial bombardments, running so fast that
> I didn't even have time to get my phone. We
> escaped in a car, first to the village of Drmbon,
> then Shushi, then Sevan. The church [here in
> Armenia] has been a life-saver, providing us with
> food and shelter. But my home is in ruins and
> I have nothing left. My brother-in-law told me
> that everything in the village has been stolen or
> demolished. He was attacked by mercenaries –
> small groups of special units – who want to take
> over the soil.
>
> I pray for peace, that I would see my husband
> again, and for my children to be able to lay
> flowers on his grave.

Angelina, aged twenty-three, described the final moments in her home.

On 26 September we had a family party in
Stepanakert. The next morning, we woke up to
the sound of bombs. I told Aram (aged 13) to get
up immediately. My husband (a military doctor)
put on his uniform and left the house.

This city was built so beautifully we couldn't
believe they would attack such a beautiful city.
But the building next to our home was hit with
Smerch [a Soviet heavy multiple rocket launcher].

We hid in the basement for four days. We
then escaped by car and asked at a random
house if we could stay with them.

I have health issues so they don't tell me the
truth about what is happening at home. I don't
know. I am worried sick. We just want peace
and recognition of Artsakh. We don't want big
houses. We can live in small houses. We just want
to return to our homes.

It was with a mixture of relief and concern that Baroness Cox
learned of the peace agreement signed on 9 November 2020,
which was brokered by Russia. The agreement represented a
compromise on the part of the people of Nagorno-Karabakh and
Armenia. It ensured that Azerbaijan committed to no obligations
on the future status of Karabakh, but was accepted by Armenia
in order to prevent further loss of life and destruction. This was
the result of the overwhelming military advantage of Turkish-
supported Azerbaijan, and the lack of international backing for
Armenia.

Despite the ceasefire, reports soon emerged of atrocities
perpetrated by Azerbaijani forces against Armenian civilian
and military prisoners of wars – including instances of torture,

beheadings, and desecrations of corpses – as well as claims that equivalent brutalities have been perpetrated by Syrian jihadist fighters, who were deployed to the frontline during the war, and who receive payment for every Armenian beheaded.

Caroline provides the distressing details.

> *During our visit, we were told that some perpetrators take over the prisoners' social media accounts and send pictures of dismembered, decapitated bodies to mothers and wives. It was our painful privilege to weep with some of these women, as they wait to hear from their husbands, brothers or sons, not knowing what might appear on their phone screens. There is real fear that prisoners are vulnerable to killings, torture, indefinite imprisonment or enslavement in Azerbaijan – as happened during the previous war in the early 1990s.*
>
> *We saw footage – verified by Amnesty International – which shows abuse and desecration of a human corpse, where members of Azerbaijani forces put the severed head of an Armenian civilian on a body of a dead animal, accompanied with insults and mockery. "You have no honour, this is how we take revenge for the blood of our martyrs" and "this is how we get revenge – by cutting heads," voices said off camera.*

To date, the perpetrators have not been held to account. As in the previous war, grave atrocities are committed with impunity. Years and years of crimes against humanity are downplayed or ignored by the international community. The sense of injustice and the depth of suffering among the local population is impossible to fathom. And at the time of this writing, there is a real fear that the escalation of hostilities may be the beginning of further and continuing aggression against Karabakh and Armenia.

Yet in the midst of grief, Baroness Cox always reminds her listeners, these courageous people do not just survive; they create beauty from the remains of their lives. Even during the darkest days of conflict, for her it has been both humbling and inspiring to witness the "Spirit of Armenia," rising like a phoenix from the ashes of death and destruction. Even while in mourning, these people declare their devotion to their land, their history and their rich culture of music, dance, and art. All this expresses their love for their families, for their faith communities, and for the breath-taking beauty of their land's rugged mountains, thick forests, fertile valleys, and crystal rivers. Love lies at the heart of their survival.

Years before the most recent conflict, the Archbishop of Nagorno-Karabakh spoke of the 1990s war in profound words, written at the height of the battle, when 400 missiles a day were raining down on his city. And he, too, recognised very well that "dignity is a crown of thorns." That very morning his own home had been bombed and reduced to rubble, and his people were dying all around him. Yet his courageous call to love resonates for all time, and for all people:

> The help of God is great and immeasurable when the human heart turns to Him with fervour. Our nation has again begun to find its faith after 70 years of Communism. Our people are praying in basements, in cellars and in the field of battle, where we have to defend our land and the lives of those who are near and dear. It is not only the perpetrators of crime and evil who commit sin,

but also those who stand by – seeing and knowing
– and who do not condemn it or try to avert it.
Blessed are the peacemakers, for they will be
called sons of God. We do not hate; we believe
in a God of love. We must love. Even if there are
demonic forces at work, not only in this conflict,
but in other parts of the world, we must still love.
We must always love. We must always love.

Caroline's father, Robert John McNeill Love, a well-regarded surgeon and author.

Baroness Cox of Queensbury.

Caroline's father served in the Royal Army Medical Corps during World War I and as a civilian surgeon during World War II. This photograph, taken in Mesopotamia, shows tents used to isolate patients he was treating for bubonic plague.

Celebrating 20 years of the Lady Cox Rehabilitation Centre in Stepanakert, an internationally-recognised centre of excellence under the inspirational leadership of the founder and director, Vardan Tadevosyan.

The Centre empowers individuals with disabilities to live independent lives, as active members of their communities.

During the 44-day war in 2020, smoke rises from an explosion behind the Centre.

Over a 6-week period between 27 September and 9 November 2020, civilians endured almost daily military offensives.

The Museum of Missing and Fallen Soldiers in Stepanakert.

The HART team lands at Agok airstrip with Benjamin Barnaba, Executive Director of the New Sudan Council of Churches.

Women in Blue Nile State call for peace, January 2013.

In the Nuba Mountains, aerial bombardments force civilians to live in snake-infested caves, January 2017.

The indestructible spirit of the Nuba Mountain people: a celebration of their traditional culture.

A village in the Blue Nile bombed by the former military regime.

An urgent visit to the village of Kolom in the disputed Abyei region on the Sudan-South Sudan border. Just hours after the massacre, homes were still burning with burnt corpses inside.

During the Kolom massacre, 32 villagers were killed.

A makeshift hut in Hai Masna IDP camp in Wau, South Sudan.

Amelia Benjamin, a Community Leader in Cathedral IDP Camp in Wau, South Sudan.

Community Health Workers from Shan Women's Action Network (SWAN).

Dr Sasa, founder of Health and Hope, appointed in 2021 as Burma's Special Envoy to the United Nations.

A camp for displaced Karen people in the aftermath of an attack by the military regime.

With Karen children in a camp for displaced people, Thai-Burma border, 1998.

Swaleen River, Thai-Burma border: illegal crossing into Burma, 1998.

Shan Women's Action Network (SWAN) 20th Anniversary Celebrations in 2019.

Dr Sasa, Vardan Tadevosyan, Pippa Gerhard, and Caroline alongside staff and patients at the Ayemyitta Rehabilitation Centre.

Children playing among the ruins in Aleppo in 2016.

Further destruction in Aleppo.

View of Maalouola, where reconstruction is taking place.

One of Maalouola's sacred shrines vandalised by Islamist extremists.

Team members of St Ephrem Patriarchal Development Committee (EPDC), empowering women in Maaloula to preserve fruits and vegetables to provide food for their families and to sell produce to generate income.

Courageous women displaced from East Gouta, near Damascus.

Caroline's message to survivors of Fulani herders' attacks in Anguldi refugee camp: "You are not forgotten".

The Anglican Bishop of Bauchi in one of his churches destroyed by Boko Haram.

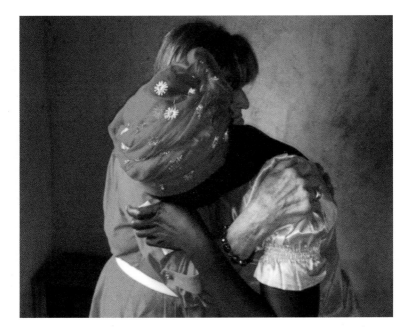

Veronica, who survived an attack by Fulani militia. She told Caroline: "They amputated my forefinger and I passed out. When I woke up, I saw my 6 year-old daughter on the ground, dead, with my chopped finger in her mouth."

With Revd David Thomas, paying respect to 7 victims at their mass grave in Zangam village, Kafanchan Diocese.

Reconciliation project in Plateau state with local Muslims and Christians.

Caroline with Archbishop Ben Kwashi and his wife Gloria.

Chapter Four

Myanmar – "Land without Evil"

In the heart of London, 10 March 2020 was another blustery day. And as Baroness Cox drove her time-worn Toyota Prius towards Westminster, she recalled that the date marked a special debate in response to International Women's Day. It pleased her that the occasion would be, as always, recognised in the House of Lords. However, as important as women's issues have always been to her, what she had to say that day would address far more extensive concerns.

As she pulled into the parking area, the attendant recognised her and grinned brightly, "G'day Milady!" "Good day to you as well," she replied, smiling warmly in return while hurriedly gathering her handbag, document files and other necessities and rushing into the stately old building.

Caroline Cox quickly made her way into the elegant Lords Chamber. And before long, she was addressing her peers about one of the concerns she very much wanted to introduce at that important session. She began her remarks:

> Please come with me to the remotest
> regions in the jungles and mountains of

Myanmar's Chin state. It is so remote that, when
a small team from HART [Humanitarian Aid Relief
Trust] visited in 2015, there were no roads. We
had to travel the last 20 hours in a jeep on a way
hacked through the jungle, with a 2,000-foot
precipice on one side and a cliff on the other—
but it was worth every minute. The region was so
inaccessible that there was no healthcare, and
childhood mortality rates were indescribably high.
It was HART's privilege to support a brave young
man, known as Dr Sasa, while he was studying
to qualify as a doctor in Armenia in order to
return to his people in Chin state and establish a
training centre for community health workers, so
that they could take life-saving healthcare to their
villages, saving the lives of eight out of 10 people
who would previously have died.

People in remote areas will die of cancer
and old age, of course, but the conditions that
cause the highest mortality rates are those such
as malaria, diarrhoea and infections from cuts
from bamboo. The community health workers
were able to prevent and treat these. Dr Sasa's
work was then supported by another small NGO,
Health & Hope; now, more than 1,000 health
workers continue to save the lives of eight out of
10 people in a catchment area of 250,000 people
in remote villages.

However, problems with maternal and child
health persisted, as childbirth was managed by
traditional birth attendants – TBAs – with no
relevant knowledge. This was not their fault; no

knowledge was available. Inevitably, maternal and infant mortality rates were tragically high, until networking established another small NGO, BirthLink; it was established by Kathy Mellor, a highly qualified neonatal nurse and specialist, and her team. They went to train the TBAs in appropriate maternity and infant care. She and her midwife colleagues often had to ride on motorbikes for 17 hours through the jungle to reach the location for training. The TBAs – many of them local elderly women, including grandmothers – have now become so clinically competent that the orphanage that cared for the numerous infants whose mothers had died in childbirth has now been closed. There is no need for it.

Hansard, 10 March 2020, vol. 802, col. 976

A journey to the "Land of Smiles"

From the Iron Curtain of Marxist totalitarianism to the iron fist of militant Islamism, Baroness Cox has travelled and spoken tirelessly about human rights under some of the world's most repressive regimes. But the story of Myanmar – also known as Burma – is singular. It is the account of a brutal dictatorship with seemingly little ideological motivation other than a psychotic drive to cling to power, silence dissent, and eradicate rivals. In the process, the Burmese people's suffering has long remained unrelieved.

In November 1994 Baroness Cox was invited to Myanmar for the first time by Dr Martin Panter, a highly regarded English doctor who had worked for years among that nation's ethnic minorities. Myanmar is the size of Texas, a scenic and colourful land of mountains and rivers. It adjoins Laos and Thailand, the other corners of the Golden Triangle – one of the world's major opium-exporting centres. Myanmar was once known as the Land of the Golden Pagodas, one of the strongest enclaves of Theravada Buddhism in all Asia.

But Caroline Cox's mission had little to do with illicit drugs or Theravada Buddhism. Her goal was to gather facts about the Karen people, a tribal minority who were being driven out of their land by Burmese troops. The Karen were locked in a war that had been raging for years and appeared to be drawing to a bitter conclusion.

Lady Cox, Dr Panter, and a team of British medics had spent the night in a mission station in the town of Chiang Mai in northern Thailand. From there they would make a voyage by longboat to the refugee camps on the borderlands, and would then enter Myanmar itself.

Many Karen converted to Christianity in the early 1800s, fought alongside the British in World War II, and faced intense persecution from 1947 when the Burmese authorities set fire to 500 Karen Christians as they worshipped in a church in Tavoy State. Today this besieged ethnic group, which makes up less than ten per cent of Myanmar's population, is being systematically driven from the country's coastal region.

Their land, in Myanmar's eastern hills and delta, was once known as Kwathoolei, roughly translated as "land of smiles" or "land without evil". The Karen are among the earliest indigenous inhabitants of Myanmar, migrating from Mongolia in the centuries around the time of Christ, hundreds of years before the Myen, who would go on to dominate the region.

The Karen cherish a unique religious heritage. From generation to generation a legend was passed down that a white man would one day arrive from a faraway land, and would reveal to the Karen the truth about the gods through the golden book that he would bring with him. Many visitors heard the legend and sought to exploit it for personal gain. But in the eighteenth century, the pioneer missionary Adoniram Judson reached the Upper Salween district of Kwathoolei and preached – from the Holy Bible he carried with him – the truth of God revealed through the Christian faith.

"Successive authoritarian governments in Rangoon have harassed, brutalised, tortured, and killed countless thousands of Karen villagers," Dr Panter explained to Caroline Cox as he briefed her about their mission. "They are liable to be murdered, raped, enslaved, and pressed into forced labour." He told her of possibly thousands of Karen tribespeople who had been killed or disabled by mines, massacres, and machine guns. "They are up against a terror regime," he continued. "Even if they flee to the refugee camps on the border, the conditions are severe and they may still be subject to attack. After some forty-six years of fighting, these peace-loving and gentle people are weary of war."

The situation in Myanmar was desperate and depressing. Caroline might well have had second thoughts about her journey, considering the research she had done before leaving England and the grim picture Dr Panter now sketched out for her. But then he told her a story. If ever there was evidence that God was protecting and encouraging a mission, it could not have been more apparent to him than during one of his own early journeys to Myanmar.

A cloud of protection

Dr Panter explained that he had been seated at a table in a jungle area, eating a simple meal with his colleagues. Their party included a member of Karen intelligence, who shocked Dr Panter to the core, informing him that the Burmese military was planning a major offensive the following day. He had solid information that an air strike would be followed by an infantry attack. This Karen agent had picked up signals on Burmese radio suggesting that two battalions of soldiers were poised to move into the very area Dr Panter and his team were about to visit. There would be an air strike by fighter planes the following morning.

Panter faced a difficult decision. Not only was he responsible for his team, but also for his daughters, Rachel, thirteen and Juliet, nine, and his three-year-old son, Nathaniel, all of whom were with him. "I'd heard more than enough times about what the Burmese soldiers do," he explained to Caroline Cox. "Not only do they rape and kill but they torture. They also use children to walk in front of the soldiers as human minesweepers. So I knew what would happen if we were captured."

Feeling shaken by the news and realising they were utterly dependent on God, the team gathered to pray. As they poured out their fears and questions to heaven, Martin felt drawn to Psalm 27. He looked it up in his Bible, then read verses 2b and 3 aloud: "when my enemies and my foes attack me, they will stumble and fall. Though an army besiege me, my heart will not fear; though war break out against me, even then will I be confident."

Encouraged, Dr Panter and his team of eye specialists decided to go ahead, along with the Panter children, to continue their mission. The next morning they set off in speedboats for a long boat ride, determined to continue their work unhindered. In the course of the day, although they heard the sound of fighter planes above the clouds, the threatened attack did not take place. And the medical mission was declared a success.

"It was only on my next visit to Myanmar", Dr Panter confided in Lady Cox, "that I found out what had actually happened."

The air strike had been scheduled to begin once the morning mist burned off – an event as dependable in that part of the world as the rising of the sun. But on that particular day, something unprecedented took place. Instead of the mists being dispersed, huge cumulus clouds began to billow up from the river until they formed a deep and impenetrable bank. Somewhere, high above, fighter bombers could be heard, circling futilely, searching for a break in the clouds. The freak weather conditions continued until the pilots' fuel ran so low that they were forced to ditch their bombs and go back to their base.

"Almost all of the bombs fell on their own troops," Panter concluded with a wry smile, "apart from one that killed two Karen chickens."

The planes had returned to Rangoon and the soldiers had withdrawn from the area.

Myanmar's beautiful, abused people

Dr Panter's story served as an affirmation for Caroline Cox that she was, indeed, in the right place. She knew a great deal about the horrific abuses in Myanmar then. But today, after many subsequent trips, she has come to a deeper understanding of the country's complex history.

Throughout decades of civil war, Myanmar's ruling military regime has inflicted systematic oppression in many regions belonging to ethnic nationals, including the predominantly Muslim Rohingya, the Buddhist Shan, and Christian Kachin peoples.

The suffering inflicted by military offensives is exacerbated by frequent violations of human rights and crimes against humanity, including widespread reports of extrajudicial killings, sexual violence, and torture. Tens of thousands are displaced and face severe insecurity. Returning IDPs (Internally Displaced Peoples) frequently discover that their land has been arbitrarily seized by the army. Many find themselves trapped in conflict areas by the military, forced to seek shelter in nearby forests without access to food, water, or medical supplies.

During her many visits to Myanmar, Caroline Cox has heard horrific stories of civilians beaten and used by the military as forced labour, farms taken from villagers, and children recruited by the military. She has also seen reports of extortion, of villages being levelled to make space for hydro projects along the rivers and land-grabbing for the expansion of mining and industrial projects. And rapes – there are so many rapes and such little accountability.

She explains,

> *Sexual exploitation, humiliation and the systematic use of rape as a weapon of war are well and widely documented. Despite numerous reports by various human rights organisations, the Burmese Army continues to subject its citizens to these practices with impunity. Although some pressure has been applied by members of the international community, the suffering of the people continues unabated – and is even escalating in scale and intensity.*

For decades stories of such abuses have abounded. Recently, Baroness Cox learned about a 26-year-old woman, from a village in Putao Township. The Kachin Women's Association Thailand (KWAT) documented that the woman was gang-raped in her farm hut by seven Burmese soldiers from Command Post 33 near Putao. To protect her identity, we'll call her Ah Mi. Married with two children, Ah Mi had gone with her husband to look after their farm.

At about 3.25 p.m., the soldiers appeared at the couple's farm hut and ordered the husband to go and buy them cigarettes. While he was away, they gang raped Ah Mi – one man held her head, and another held her legs apart. They raped her, one after the other. When the husband returned at about 4.15 p.m., the soldiers threatened they would kill him if he reported the rape. They said, "Even if you tell other people, there is no one who will take action. We have the authority to rape women." The couple reported the crime to the head of their village, but he did nothing. Unsurprisingly, Ah Mi fell seriously ill after the incident.

Beautiful nation, tragic history

Over many years, Lady Cox has heard countless similar, horrific stories of civilians killed, tortured, used as forced labour, their farms stolen, and their children abducted.

Since the early 1990s, over a million Rohingya refugees (who are a stateless Muslim minority) have fled violence in successive waves of displacement. The most recent exodus began in 2017, when violence broke out in Rakhine State, with villages burned, executions, tortures, and mass rape, which drove more than 740,000 to seek refuge in Bangladesh. Over 6,700 Rohingya, including at least 730 children under the age of five, were killed in the month after the violence broke out, according to medical charity Médecins Sans Frontières (Doctors Without Borders) in its survey of 12 December 2017.

Baroness Cox is among the world's most vocal campaigners to reinstate the Rohingya's rights of citizenship. She continues to highlight concerns over their plight and to urge the international community to end impunity for crimes against humanity. However, for four decades, her advocacy initiatives in Myanmar have primarily focused on support for ethnic minorities in Chin, Shan, Kachin, and Karen States, where victims of government abuse have received considerably less international media coverage then the Rohingya refugees. And to this day, they remain desperately in need of humanitarian aid.

How did the situation become so dire? The seeds of today's nearly indescribable human rights situation in Myanmar were planted during Myanmar's years under the authority of the British empire, starting in the early nineteenth century. In those days Britain ruled India, and when several Burmese military excursions entered colonial Indian territory, the British eventually subdued Myanmar (then known as Burma) and recast it as a province of India – a Crown colony.

The situation wasn't all bad. Under British rule, the Burmese enjoyed elements of success particularly in rice exports, and their economy began to flourish. However, at the same time existing ethnic tensions were exacerbated, as the British showed a preference for Indians in the administration of the country, while they steered Christian Karen people into the army. This led to protests against the British and an atmosphere of unrest.

In the 1930s, the nation was rocked by a peasant uprising followed by a student strike organised by a young man named Aung San. In 1937 Britain agreed to the separation of the then Burma from India and to partial self-government. Then, in 1941, a wave of anti-British nationalism ushered in another empire: the Japanese "Empire of the Rising Sun". The Burma Independence Army, founded by Aung San, fought alongside the Japanese to drive the British out of Burma. But when Japan's promise of freedom proved false, Aung San established the Anti-

Fascist People's Freedom League (AFPFL) and resorted to helping the British regain control of his country. Ultimately, the Japanese were defeated at a showdown near the Irrawaddy river.

That year, 1945, General Aung San fathered a daughter, Aung San Suu Kyi. When she was two years old, her father was assassinated on the brink of achieving his dream of an independent Burma. When Aung San died, another dream died as well – that of a federal Burmese constitution offering equal status to ethnic minorities.

A fallen star

On 4 January 1948 Burma was granted full independence from Britain. As the dominant Burmese sought to impose an artificial national unity on 135 disparate ethnic-racial groups, the historic freedoms of those ethnic minorities were ignored. The new socialist parliamentary democracy found itself embroiled in a civil war with the Karen National Liberation Army, the Karenni, the Mon, and the communists.

A series of regimes came and went until late summer 1987, when angry students flooded the streets of Rangoon. The following spring, workers rioted. Students demonstrating at "White Bridge" across Inya Lake were beaten to death by riot police. Forty-two of them were rounded up and locked in a waiting van, where they were left to suffocate.

On 8 August the army was ordered to restore order; they began to shoot into the crowds. Across Burma, as many as 10,000 unarmed demonstrators were gunned down while an estimated 700,000 fled the country. Still, public protests and calls for democracy continued. Multi-party elections were promised within three months. But democracy was not the result. What the Burmese people got instead was a military coup.

General Saw Maung seized power on 18 September 1988. He suspended the constitution, imposed martial law, and transferred authority to the Orwellian-sounding State Law and Order Restoration Council (SLORC).

The junta claimed it was providing a new beginning. Burma's name was changed to Myanmar and its capital, Rangoon, became Yangon. Steps were taken to liberalise the economy, even to stage democratic elections – but with an ominous twist. The leader of the opposing National League for Democracy, Aung San Suu Kyi, daughter of the late Aung San, was placed under house arrest. Nevertheless, her party won a landslide victory at the elections in May 1990, claiming eighty-two per cent of the parliamentary seats.

Despite the election's clear mandate, however, nothing changed. The military, whose party had gained just ten per cent of the vote, refused to recognise the election results and arrested many of the elected politicians. Thousands of pro-democracy activists were interrogated, tortured, and imprisoned. The International Committee of the Red Cross later withdrew from Myanmar because the government would not permit private access to prisoners.

In 1991 Aung San Suu Kyi, who had drawn her inspiration from the non-violent protests of Martin Luther King and Mahatma Gandhi, was awarded the Nobel Peace Prize. Meanwhile, a military crackdown began against the Christian Karen and the Muslim-led pro-independence movement. Within a year more than 100,000 Muslims were to flee the country. But Suu Kyi was widely looked upon as the great hope of freedom for the Burmese people.

By 2006, Suu Kyi had been under house arrest or imprisoned for ten of the last sixteen years. After 2004 she was nearly incommunicado, although in November 2006 she was permitted a rare visit by a United Nations Under-Secretary. Major news sources reported that her spirits were strong; her health was described as good, though she was in need of regular medical care.

Suu Kyi was long seen as a great human rights hero by the Burmese population. She was released from house arrest in 2010 and was promptly elected and sworn in as a Member of Parliament in 2012.

Sadly, however, after becoming Myanmar's State Counsellor in 2015, her star began to fall. On her watch, religious nationalism and intolerance grew. She remained silent in the face of atrocity crimes and defended the military's genocidal campaign against the Rohingyas. Although a decade of reforms have increased space for civil society and the media, any hopes that democracy would lead to genuine peace seem far off. The military coup of February 2021 sets things back even further. At the time of writing, Myanmar risks returning to pariah status.

Listening carefully, responding wholeheartedly

Caroline Cox's 1994 trip with Dr Panter launched the beginning of her heartfelt engagement with Myanmar's abused people, and that effort that has continued ever since. In the years following that first encounter, her determination to focus attention to Myanmar's human rights violations has deepened with every passing year. She is particularly sensitive to the needs of Myanmar's minority populations who suffer the most at the hands of the ruling regime.

Today, the refugee camps dotting the Thai-Burmese border remain home to untold thousands of Burmese minorities who have been driven from their homes and sources of income by undisciplined and unscrupulous attacks, nearly all at the hands of the Burmese Army. The camps house refugees in rudimentary structures on stilts, with thatched roofs and thin woven walls through which unshaded sunlight streams. There is no shortage of camps to visit and no scarcity of victims to tell their stories. And the people Baroness Cox has reached out to in those camps – as well as inside Myanmar's borders – have frequently expressed both their concerns about their shocking conditions and their gratitude to her and HART.

In the words of Ying Lao, an advisory member of SWAN (Shan Women's Action Network), "You showed us light in a time of darkness, hope in a time of despair and most importantly, you gave us the unbreakable bond of sisterhood."

During her trips inside Myanmar and across the border into Thailand's refugee camps, Caroline Cox can be found sitting for hours, an interpreter by her side, interviewing refugees and filling up notebook after notebook. Each of her reports confirms the ones that preceded it, entailing horrible cases of rape, torture, and abduction of villagers. These assaults include the very elderly, alongside pregnant women and small children. Many of these innocents are used as slave labourers and human minesweepers. And they exist in poverty – such gripping poverty.

A healthcare director described a recent case.

> One lady did not inform us that she was pregnant and due to give birth. After she gave birth at midnight, a colleague received an urgent call at 5 a.m. because the placenta was not coming out. The mother was in distress, had lost a lot of blood and was very pale. The medical worker urgently needed to get the mother to a hospital but it was

rainy season and they needed a good car. After
finding a car but no driver, my distraught colleague
(with only a learner's licence!) took matters into her
own hands and also provided money at her own
risk to ensure the mother was seen upon arrival.
Amazingly, the new mother survived.

Since her first visit, Baroness Cox has spoken about these
atrocities not only in the House of Lords, but also at small
church groups, elite military conferences, and in television
interviews. She has never stopped speaking as an eyewitness to
Myanmar's sorrows.

Most recently, Baroness Cox and HART have concentrated
their energies on promoting several promising projects.

Caroline is enthusiastic about SWAN, located in Taunggyi,
Shan State, which coordinates a number of programmes relating
to health, education, and women's empowerment, as well as
conducting advocacy and research. HART is the primary donor for
SWAN's health programme, the Women's Wellbeing Programme,
aimed to reduce maternal, infant, and child mortality rates in
rural areas of Shan State and among displaced populations in
Thailand.

Another project is Loi Tai Leng School, where 700 students
attend, in one of six displacement camps along the Thai-Myanmar
border. HART was motivated by funding cuts in October 2017 to
start supporting this school, with the help of London's Palmers
Green High School.

More than half the children who attend Loi Tai Leng
School board there, either because they have been orphaned
or abandoned during the ongoing conflict, or because they live
in remote areas far from the school and the journey is far too
dangerous to manage every day.

Education is extremely important to these children, as success in exams provides their ticket to study at a university in Thailand and access to legal work. Shan/Burmese people are not officially recognised as refugees in Thailand, which forces many migrants into dangerous and illegal work to make money to feed their families.

HART's original partner Doh Say and his team regularly cross the border from Thailand into Myanmar to take life-saving medicine and provide basic healthcare within areas of Myanmar that experience conflict. These courageous workers are mainly active within the Karenni State, offering assistance to Karenni and Karen people who travel across the state border to receive medical care. HART supported Doh Say by funding the medicines he transported across the border to treat patients as well as equipment for his mobile clinics. He now works with the inspirational organisation FBR (Free Burma Rangers).

In Chin State the Health and Hope project is led by Dr Taing Saing San – better known as Dr SaSa. He is the first and only qualified medical doctor in Chin state. HART has been supporting Dr SaSa since 2005, and his Health and Hope outreach since it was founded in 2009, prior to which there was almost no healthcare available in Chin State. At the heart of Health and Hope's work is the training of Community Health Workers (CHWs) which is a participatory approach to healthcare, deeply rooted in local communities. In 2014, 157 new CHWs were trained, bringing the total number trained up to 838, with 473 villages now benefitting from the activities of a trained CHW. These CHWs are estimated to save the lives of as many as eight out of ten people who would previously have died.

On another important and unique front, since 2018 HART has sought to connect the knowledge and expertise of HART partner Vardan Tadevosyan in Nagorno-Karabakh with that of HART's Burmese partners. Since 1999, Baroness Cox has supported Vardan as he provides disability rehabilitation in a once bomb-damaged school building that he has transformed into an internationally recognised Centre of Excellence. Vardan has trained more than sixty staff to provide therapeutic services for more than 1,000 people per year suffering from both physical and psychological disabilities (such as infants with cerebral palsy and Down's Syndrome, to children with autism and elderly people having who have suffered strokes). Vardan's experience in providing such education in a post-conflict zone qualifies him uniquely to provide care for the disabled in Myanmar for whom such provision has never been available.

Myanmar: bombs into bells

As we've seen, Baroness Cox's heart holds a special place for Myanmar, where she has worked both among the suffering people there, and with those who have been displaced and who are now in the refugee camps across the Thai border. She describes one unforgettable impression.

> *I will never forget walking through one camp soon after it had suffered a raid, feeling darkness like that of the blackened landscape around me: huts burnt, everything destroyed. We entered the remains of a hut and encountered what I can only call a miracle of grace. Ma Su, a 38-year-old Karen lady whose home was destroyed by shelling, was also shot by a soldier running rampage through the camp. She is recovering from her wounds, but still in pain. When we asked her what she felt about the soldier who*

shot her so gratuitously, her reply was both simple
and wholehearted: "I love him. The Bible tells us to
love our enemies – so of course I love him: he is my
brother."

What a glorious example of Christ's redeeming
love which can transform brutality and suffering into
redemptive, forgiving love.

I will never forget another occasion when we had
walked across the border into Myanmar, and climbed
up a steep mountain to meet some of the internally
displaced people (IDPs is the jargon phrase) living in
primitive conditions in constant fear of bombardment.
Their little camp had been bombed three times in
the last few months. As we approached them, feeling
totally inadequate to begin to address the enormity of
their needs, they came running to us with tears in their
eyes, crying:

"Thank God you have come. We thought the world
had forgotten us. But the fact that you are here makes
all the difference: to know that we are not forgotten
gives us the strength to continue to struggle to survive.
It wouldn't matter if you brought nothing with you –
the fact that you are here is all that matters."

On our way down the mountain from our
encounter with this besieged, bombarded and
vulnerable little Karen community, we suddenly
heard a sound which resembled that of a church bell.
Intrigued, we followed the sound and found a little
worshipping Baptist church. We also found that
the bell which had summoned us was a Burmese
bombshell, lovingly transformed into a single
chime. I thought to myself, in today's world, instead

*of swords into ploughshares, we have bombs
into bells.*

*The bombs continue to fall on innocent civilians
– Christian, Buddhist, animist and Muslim. Please
pray that soon there will be a political solution in
favour of democracy, that the bombs will cease, and
that the church bells will ring in celebration for
peace with justice for all the people of Myanmar.*

Pastor Simon – "In the hands of God"

In her 2006 book *Cox's Book of Modern Saints and Martyrs*,
Baroness Cox writes about a man for whom she has deep
admiration – Pastor Simon, who has since sadly died. He
was a Karen who fled for his life from Myanmar and for many
years served God and his countrymen from a refugee camp in
Thailand. She writes,

> To anyone else, Pastor Simon's circumstances are
> bleak, but he has transformed the deprivations of
> life in a camp for the displaced from a situation
> of despair into a place of hope. He has established
> a theological seminary in the camps and cares
> for many Karen children, including orphans who
> have had to flee from their homes in Myanmar in
> order to survive.

Pastor Simon's perspective on the troubles around him is both
humbling and heartbreaking with such powerful imagery in his
fifth language. He gave Baroness Cox this meditation on one of
her visits:

They call us a displaced people,
But praise God, we are not misplaced.
They say they see no hope for our future,
But praise God, our future is as bright as the
    promises of God.
They say the life of our people is a misery,
But praise God, our life is a mystery.
For what they say is what they see,
And what they see is temporal.
But ours is the eternal.
All because we put ourselves,
In the hands of God we trust.

Chapter Five

Nigeria – "Will You Tell the World?"

Nigerian Archbishop Ben's beautiful smile is a kind of miracle. It's hard to imagine that a man with such a radiant, joyful countenance could have looked upon as much suffering as he has. And yet, like so many of Nigeria's beleaguered Christians, the Rt Revd Dr Benjamin Argak Kwashi somehow manages to find happiness and serenity in the midst of devastating circumstances. Like the beloved "Bishop Ben", Nigeria's believers are an inspiration in the midst of their distress, which is both intense and intensifying.

Archbishop Ben Kwashi was born in 1955, studied at the Theological College of Northern Nigeria and was ordained in 1982. He has served in Christian ministry in both rural and urban areas, working tirelessly and faithfully. In 1987 his church and home were burned to the ground in Christian-Muslim riots. In 1992 he was consecrated and enthroned as Bishop of Jos, and in 2008 he was consecrated as Archbishop of Jos. Under his leadership several schools, a Christian Institute, and healthcare programmes have been established, including special care for a very large number of HIV/AIDS patients along with both Muslim and Christian orphans. Archbishop Ben is married to Gloria Ladi Kwashi, and they have six children.

Caroline expresses special admiration and affection for Gloria. "She is always ready to help when a village is attacked, filling a bus with clothes, cooking pots – whatever is needed – and driving into the troubled areas. My nickname for her is 'Gloria in Excelsis'."

Gloria's concern for those attacked by terrorists came close to home in February 2006, when jihadis broke into the Kwashis' own house. They weren't just interested in robbery or vandalism – their intention was to murder then Bishop Ben. He was not at home, so they attacked his family instead. They savagely beat two of his sons, one so fiercely that he lost consciousness. But they saved their worst violence for Gloria. They sexually assaulted her. They beat her. They subjected her to such severe torture that she lost her eyesight temporarily. Before leaving, the assailants also attacked members of the bishop's staff and stole significant amounts of money belonging to the diocese.

When Bishop Ben was notified of the cruelty meted out to his family – an attack that was intended for him – he rushed back to Jos. Ben's immediate message to friends abroad was a request to the authorities to provide adequate security for his community. The next day, his subsequent messages were profoundly inspiring examples of forgiveness, resilience, and courage. He wrote:

> We have been surrounded by love, support and
> prayers. Last night, I had a good laugh at myself
> when I just sat down and thought about my
> life... My life and that of my family seems to be
> in constant danger and inviting the prayers of
> the church of God around the world. Maybe I
> should get into more trouble..!! The testimony
> of the recent happenings is the miraculous
> healing that the prayer of the church has

brought upon Gloria, myself, the children and the entire diocese. Her recovery is remarkable... the surgery was a huge success. She is healing steadily, and she was able to sit down to take Holy Communion last night. Her speech is restored even though it is a bit slow and weak... We are praying that our sufferings, and specifically that the humiliation, blood, tears and pains of Gloria, may bring tremendous glory to God...

"You are an answer to our prayers"

Baroness Cox's first visit to Nigeria took place in 1998, shortly after an Anglican conference at Lambeth Palace, the Archbishop of Canterbury's headquarters, from which many African clergy and bishops returned to their homes feeling demoralised and alienated. In Jos, during her first conversation with Bishop Ben, Lady Cox asked him if he and his brother bishops felt that the Anglican Church had any real feeling for the persecuted church. For a moment, he lost his happy smile. "No. I and my brother bishops feel very sad and alone," he admitted. "Indeed, we felt so alone that we turned to God and said our prayers – which, perhaps, being bishops, we should have done already."

Then he asked Baroness Cox a life-changing question: "But now you have come. You are an answer to our prayers. Will you tell the world what is happening here in Nigeria?"

Subsequently, Baroness Cox did just that – and she has done so ever since. Through her organisation, HART, life-saving resources have been sent to people suffering from the conflicts in Jos and elsewhere in the country. She describes an early blessing.

*We continue to be amazed to see relatively small
sums of money used in ways which exceed any
expectations. For example, one English country
church gave a generous donation of £2,000. I
decided to dedicate the entire amount to one place, so
I asked the vicar to select one of the areas where we
are working. Nigeria was chosen. A few months later,
our HART team visited Jos and asked to see how the
church's donation had been used. The £2,000 had
been used to rebuild four churches and three schools.*

Late one evening Caroline Cox visited the remote village where
that church's money had been put to use in rebuilding a local
church that had been destroyed. She received a rapturous
welcome. Villagers appeared, seemingly out of nowhere, their
smiles lighting up the darkness. One of them told her:

We have lost everything in this conflict, and
we were in despair. We had no idea how we
were ever going to rebuild anything, including
our precious church. Then we suddenly heard
that you were coming. We learned that people
far away loved us and cared enough to help us
rebuild our community. We are so grateful! And
now we have a building, new people are coming
to join us and our church family is growing.

Caroline returned to Britain on a Friday evening. On Saturday, she
downloaded her photos onto PowerPoint; on Sunday morning
she was back in that same English country church's pulpit,
showing the pictures and saying a heartfelt "Thank you" to the
congregation for the difference they had made to these people

so far away. "The Nigerians thought they had been forgotten," she recalls, "but instead had learned that there are people who do love and care for them." The generous congregation was deeply moved – and promptly gave another £4,000 – which Caroline quickly sent to then Bishop Ben.

The battle over Shari'a law

Nigeria is Africa's most populous nation, nearly equally divided between Muslims and Christian, with most Muslims located in the country's northern states. Those states have been ravaged by conflict for decades, which is frequently associated with religious issues. Brutality and bloodshed have increased dramatically during the past twenty years, partly due to the imposition of harsh interpretations of Shari'a (Islamic) law. Christians, along with many peaceable Muslims and others, have resisted this radical Islamist agenda with great determination, and their resistance has often led to violence. It is estimated that as many as 60,000 women, men, and children have perished over past decades, many of them Christians. There has also been a massive destruction of property.

Since 1999, twelve Nigerian states have formally implemented Shari'a law, and their radical leaders will accept no alternative to Islam's strict legal system. Their reasons are explained succinctly by author and historian Mervyn Hiskett, who writes in his 1994 book *The Sword of Truth*:

> Islam has been emphatic that any aspect of
> culture that is inconsistent with the Sacred Law
> has no legitimacy and should not be considered
> binding on society... Indeed, Islam does not

accept that people should have customs or
traditions other than religious ones; for if Allah's
way is a comprehensive way of life, what room is
there for custom and tradition?

Since those twelve states have adopted Shari'a law, alongside the present violence in the country, in today's Nigeria there is a great sense of foreboding among the Christian community. There is fear that if, and when, Shari'a has been extended to nineteen of Nigeria's thirty-six states, it could then be possible to change the constitution so that Nigeria itself would become an Islamic nation. The impact of this on the non-Muslim population especially would be catastrophic.

Wherever strict interpretations of Shari'a rules apply, Christians (and Jews – both are identified as "People of the Book") are assigned *dhimmi* status. According to traditional Islam, a *dhimmi* is a second- or third-class citizen who implicitly acknowledges the supremacy of Muslim rule, pays a special tax (*jizya*), and has far fewer legal rights than Muslims. During a meeting with Lady Cox in the early 2000s, leaders of a Shari'a court in Kano acknowledged that it is perfectly acceptable Islamic practice to deceive or defraud Christians in any way deemed necessary to further the cause of Islam. According to their understanding of the Shari'a system, any reassurances or promises given to "People of the Book" could be broken with moral impunity. She describes the event:

*We were received by the acting Chief Kadir of the
Shari'a Court in Kano, the Chief Registrar Mr Ismail
Ahad. Mr Ismail claimed that the implementation
of Shari'a law was nothing new in Kano. It had
been implemented in pre-colonial days – except, he*

> *explained, for those parts of the criminal aspects of the law that called for amputations and other extreme physical punishments. These had not been allowed previously. Now, however, the full Shari'a was being implemented... the Chief Registrar repeated more than once that Shari'a operates only for Muslims, and that he could never envisage the possibility of full Shari'a in Nigeria. But he did admit that "Shari'a is above all and over all and is in fact above the Constitution. Within five years we will amend the constitution for Shari'a law."*

The application of these discriminatory Shari'a law principles has been associated with escalating religious persecution. In some cases, special religious police, Hisbah, have been trained to enforce Shari'a law. They have no legal status under Nigerian law, and although they are not properly constituted police, they are permitted by state governments to arrest, jail, and intimidate. They are also seen as agents of coercion, intimidation, and harassment.

Jihad in Nigeria

On one of her early trips to Nigeria, Caroline Cox visited Kassa, a village outside Jos. For years, Muslims and Christians had lived peacefully together there. But, little by little, Muslims who lived in the village began to sell their houses to their Christian neighbours, and eventually they had nearly all relocated elsewhere. Just after midnight on an October night, armed tribesmen attacked the village assisted by mercenaries, possibly from Chad and Niger. According to the villagers, the attack was carefully planned and systematic. The armed men invaded from three different directions. The houses that had been sold to Christians by Muslims were specifically targeted for burning. Those who lived in them had virtually no warning of the attack.

Most of the villagers were sound asleep when they suddenly heard gunshots and men shouting "*Allah-u-Akbar*!" The jihadis converged on the village, shooting randomly. As the terrified victims fled into the surrounding bushes, their assailants doused their houses with petrol, set light to them, and burned them to the ground. Five villagers were killed in the attack, including one old man who was murdered in his house. Another man died trying to stop the attackers from destroying his shop, along with a woman and a child. When the attack began, a few of the villagers drove their cars to the local police station, assuming the vehicles would be safe under police protection. But the police also fled once the attack was under way. The jihadis not only outnumbered them but were also far better armed. Meanwhile, all the cars that were in the police compound were torched and destroyed.

A 40-year-old woman, Chundung Danielle, was sleeping in her hut with her husband and children when the sound of gunshots awakened them all. Her husband panicked and fled the house, leaving Danielle alone with their children. She was nine months pregnant at the time. A gang of terrorists burst into the house and demanded that she tell them where her husband was.

"He's not here... he ran away," she cried.

In response, the attackers started beating her and the children, brandishing knives. One cautioned the others, "We aren't supposed to attack women and children!"

At his word, most of them retreated. But two of the thugs were unmoved – they slashed at the mother and children with their knives. Then, for good measure, one of them shot Danielle in the stomach. They left her bleeding and in a grave condition. Not until the next morning was she rushed to hospital, where she underwent emergency surgery. Her baby was delivered alive, but has since died.

A few years later, a serious outbreak of violence erupted in Namu after a Christian boy was killed. Caroline Cox also visited that village and learned that the trouble had begun over the allocation of land. While the quarrelling continued, the local emir quietly gathered a group of mercenaries, but carefully kept them out of sight. Then the Christian boy was murdered. Fighting immediately broke out, and it suddenly erupted into large-scale violence when the mercenaries joined the fray.

On this occasion, however, the main casualties were the mercenaries themselves. Their commander was killed and his soldiers apparently lost their way and could not escape. At least sixty people lost their lives (some estimate that the number could have been as high as 200), and there were many more casualties. Numerous properties were burned, the majority of them belonging to Christians. There is still widespread tension in Namu, and fear of further violence. Small-scale but serious incidents continue to occur with disturbing frequency.

In yet another confrontation in June 2006, armed robbers attacked a home on the campus of Jos State University. Canon Emmanuel Ajulo was dining at home with his family when the assailants broke into the house, robbed and looted the premises, and then fled. Ajulo claims that the police took no effective action.

The Ajulo incident is not an aberration. Nigerian Christian communities across the country report a long-standing failure of the police to take effective action to prevent or respond to attacks. A prime example comes from Archbishop Ben Kwashi himself. Although the police were telephoned immediately when his wife and family were so savagely assaulted, three hours passed before any officers arrived on the scene. Local leaders argue that both state and federal governments are appeasing the militants, and their refusal to take appropriate measures is causing mounting frustration in the Christian communities. They also claim that, on occasions when Christians do defend themselves, police arrest the Christians and blame them for being the aggressors. This pattern has not changed, and reportedly continues unabated until today.

Devastation in Kano State

Caroline Cox first learned about the danger faced by Christians in Kano State during a visit to the Anglican bishop of Kano, the Rt Revd Zakka Lalle Nyam. Along with other local leaders, Bishop Nyam revealed story after story of Christians who had been killed and churches that had been destroyed. "They assured me," she said later, "that a Muslim who kills a Christian pastor receives a 'reward' of a sum equivalent to a month's average wage."

Bishop Nyam later distributed a report about riots that had taken place in Kano. He wrote, "It is estimated that well over 3,000 people were killed and property worth over 500 million nyra destroyed... Most, if not all, church buildings at Panshakara, Shagari quarters, Zango, Brigade, Namibia, Sheka and Challawa and some in Badawa were all burnt down." Bishop Nyam's report continued:

> Some of the stories that happened are too
> inhuman to tell. [They are so appalling that
> readers may find them hard to believe, and we
> quote only those we learned from respected and

reputable sources. And although they may seem exaggerated beyond belief to those unfamiliar with such situations, they are, tragically, not untypical.] For example, at Sharada, a seven-day-old baby belonging to a Tyoruba family was said to have been fried alive in boiling oil on the day of its christening. The parents had invited guests to the naming ceremony of the poor child and when this was taking place the militants arrived and attacked. Everyone took to his or her heels, leaving the baby (who was in the house calmly sleeping) to the mercy of the jihadists. Without qualms... the child was picked up and thrown into the boiling oil; as it continued to whine until it died the jihadists danced round the pot chanting and shrieking in an obscene way and brandishing their weapons... [This story was told by a guest who begged to remain anonymous.]

These brutalities took place against a backdrop of systematic oppression and deliberate targeting of Christians. Compared with such violence, incidents of discrimination can seem innocuous, but they bear witness to the disdain with which Christians are treated in Kano State. For example, the first Anglican church built in Kano, at Fagge, was overcrowded, and the then primate of the Anglican Communion, Archbishop Robert Runcie, laid the foundation stone of a new church on 29 April 1982. The building was partially erected, but then the government forbade further development. The reason given – and this explanation was given only verbally – was that Muslims worshipping in an adjacent mosque, which had been built long after the church was founded, would be offended by the sight of a church while praying. It would be impossible to build a wall sufficiently high to shield them from the sight of the church as they lifted their eyes towards heaven in prayer. To this day, the church remains only partially built. A committee of inquiry has been established, but no report has yet been published.

As the Bishop of Kano carefully explained, "They do not make it easy for us to live with them."

Another more distressing issue, especially in areas under the jurisdiction of Shari'a courts, concerns the problems facing Muslims who convert to Christianity. Having committed apostasy, as defined in Islamic law, their lives are at risk – at the hands of their own families and communities; they call it "honour killing". If they run away and seek sanctuary elsewhere, they are still in danger of being hunted down, typically by young zealots who kill them, sometimes by decapitation.

Those who are not killed are often taken away with the intention of reconverting them to Islam. Christian churches spend a great amount of time and resources providing such persons with protection and the opportunity to develop a new life. It is important to remember that these converts have exercised a fundamental freedom – to change their religious beliefs – in accordance with the Universal Declaration of Human Rights, to which Nigeria is a signatory.

Despite all these challenges, Bishop Nyam emphasised the resilience of the Nigerian Christian church and the resolve of individual believers. Christian churches continue to grow in size and number. "If they kill 200 Christian people and destroy a church," he says with a solemn smile, "within a few years, there will be 200 more Christians – for the blood of the martyrs is the seed of the church."

Boko Haram, ISWAP, and Fulani militia

Since those early days of Baroness Cox's engagement with Nigeria, the precarious situation of Christians has gone from bad to far worse. As years have passed, two notorious groups have emerged and perpetrated enormous levels of death and violence. The best known are Boko Haram and an ISIS affiliate: the Islamic State in West Africa Province (ISWAP). Their attacks have primarily taken place in Nigeria's north-east states, especially in Borno, Yobe, and Gombe, many against Muslims who do not subscribe to their radical ideology. But they are not limited to that area and have afflicted other parts of the country as well.

The evolution of Boko Haram terrorism began when a charismatic cleric Mohammed Yusuf formed Boko Haram in Maiduguri in 2002. He set up a religious complex, which included a mosque and an Islamic school. After Mohammed Yusuf was killed by Nigerian authorities, the group – along with other smaller jihadi sects – became more murderous.

On 25 December 2011, the BBC reported that a series of church bombings had killed nearly forty worshippers in the Abuja area:

> A series of bomb attacks in Nigeria, including two on Christmas Day church services, have left almost 40 people dead and many injured. The Islamist group Boko Haram said it carried out the attacks, including one on St Theresa's Church in Madalla, near the capital Abuja, that killed 35. National Emergency Management Agency (Nema) spokesman Yushau Shuaibu told the BBC that the latest Abuja explosion had happened in the street outside the

> church. He said the church – which can hold
> up to 1,000 people – had been badly affected
> by the blast.

By 2014, the Boko Haram "brand" became broadly recognisable worldwide after their kidnapping of 276 girls from a Chibok school. At that time, US First Lady Michelle Obama launched a *#bringbackourgirls* campaign to draw attention to their plight.

Unfortunately, Boko Haram and ISWAP are not alone in their brutality. An additional and increasingly deadly terror group is frequently identified as the Fulani militia – a sub-group of well-armed individuals of Fulani ethnicity who carry out attacks in order to seize property and pastureland from predominantly Christian communities. The Global Terrorism Index in 2016 and 2017 named Fulani militia as the fourth deadliest terrorist group in the world. In the process of their land-grabs, they have been known to kill, rape, torch homes and churches, while kidnapping girls, women, and boys. Their attacks have principally taken place in Nigeria's Middle Belt, but not exclusively so.

Living in fear – for good reason

On 15 July 2020 a *Christian Post* headline reported that 1,202 Nigerian Christians had been killed in the first six months of 2020. This was in addition to 11,000 Christians that Genocide Watch claimed to have been killed since June 2015. Today, such violence has reached a point at which expert observers and analysts are warning of a potential genocide – a "slow-motion war" across Africa's largest and most economically powerful nation.

Baroness Cox described one of the attacks, following a visit to Plateau State.

> *We visited four villages in the Rapp district, Plateau State: Loboring; Jong; Rabuk; and Zim – all within two square miles of each other. In 2015, Fulani militia massacred 21 of the villagers here. We stood in the rubble of a pastor's home where he had been slaughtered. Although the sun was beginning to set, our guide was keen for us to meet a handful of families who had chosen to return, either to bury their dead or rebuild their homes. It was an unforgettable visit.*
>
> *The scenery there is beautiful. I am told the red soil is perfect for growing carrots. "That is where they camped before the attack," the local pastor points to a steep hill. "Men dressed in black. They were trained terrorists, killing those who couldn't run." We are looking at buildings that have been smashed to pieces. The surrounding farmland is now occupied by Fulani herders, including their cattle.*
>
> *We arrive at the fourth village before dark, giving us time to explore the rubble and shake hands with villagers. Our guide looks agitated. He ushers us to return to the minibus, so we amble on board and hit the road. I say "road". It's not really a road. Barely a track. At one point, still in the Rapp district, the van hits a rock and almost gets stuck in a ditch. But it's the only way out so that's the route we take.*
>
> *Half an hour later, gunmen emerge from the hills, block the road and start shooting at passing vehicles. Automatic rifles. AK47s. It is an ambush*

*and we know that we are the target, though
thankfully our minibus has already left the valley,
just in time.*

Such stories about the assaults in Nigeria are rarely reported in mainstream media outlets, and instead are generally found in publications sponsored by Christian non-profit organisations in their newsletters and websites. For this reason, the genocidal intentions of Boko Haram, ISWAP, and Fulani jihadis don't seem to have gained enough attention to sufficiently alarm global powers and authorities. To make matters far worse, when and if these incidents are reported – especially reports of attacks by Fulani radicals – they are regularly explained away as effects of climate change, local feuds, resources, or internecine religious wars for which both sides bear equal responsibility. It is true that causes of violence are specific to the local area's history, politics, ethno-linguistic make-up, and resource competition. But far too little attention is paid to very obvious religious factors – and sometimes none at all.

It wasn't until the end of 2020 that the US State Department designated Nigeria as a "Country of Particular Concern" for violations of religious freedom. During a special briefing on 8 December, US Ambassador-at-Large for International Religious Freedom Sam Brownback said:

> The world has great concern about what's taking place in Nigeria at this time, and a number of terrorist groups are organizing and pushing into the country. We're seeing a lot of religious-tinged violence taking place in that country and indeed in West Africa. It's an area of growing concern about what's happening, in particular the tension

> that's taking place there between religious groups.
> And it's often the religious affiliation is used to try
> to recruit and inspire violent acts.

No doubt one reason among many for the US Ambassador's statement was a horrifying incident in which two Catholic priests and more than a dozen of their parishioners had been murdered. It was reported that Father Joseph Gor and Father Felix Tyolaha of St Ignatius Catholic Church had been attacked during a morning Mass in April 2018. Prior to being murdered, Father Gor had written on Facebook: "Living in fear. The Fulani herdsmen are still around us in Mbalom. They refuse to go. They still go grazing around us. No weapons to defend ourselves...."

Later that year the European Centre for Law and Justice later filed an official request asking the UN to "recognise and put an end to the atrocities being carried about against Christians in Nigeria."

Another document had been presented to the UN's Human Rights Council in August 2018, urging that it step in and stop the slaughter of Christians in Nigeria, especially the violence perpetrated by the extremist Boko Haram group. "Increasingly," that communique warned, "Nigeria has become home to radical groups that seek to eliminate Christianity from the country."

Also that year, Open Doors – a well-established and trustworthy watchdog organisation – reported that a dozen Christian villages had been completely wiped out in a four-day massacre.

> Most of the victims were in their homes sleeping
> when the attacks began... when Muslim Fulani
> militant herdsmen began their killing spree...

In only days, a dozen villages in Nigeria's
Plateau state were wiped out.... As many as
200 Christians had been killed, however, some
residents fear the death toll may be even higher,
as more bodies are yet to be recovered, while
others were burned beyond recognition.

"Behind every statistic is a human horror story"

Despite reports of ever-increasing danger, in her determination
to assist some of Nigeria's most vulnerable communities,
Baroness Cox returned to the country to interview victims and
document their appalling experiences.

She described her visit, in part, for her HART supporters:

> *In November, I met survivors of five villages attacked
> by Fulani militia, forcing an estimated 12,000
> people to flee. In two of the villages, 116 people
> were killed. It was possible to meet only a limited
> number of survivors, but the consistency of their
> experiences is deeply disturbing and consistent with
> evidence from numerous previous visits. These are
> disturbing statistics, but behind every statistic is a
> human horror story. I give just a few examples of
> the suffering of the people: sadly, I could massively
> multiply them.*
>
> *Antonia from Karamai said: "I saw my brother-
> in-law's body on the ground, hacked to pieces by a
> machete. Our home was destroyed. The hospital was
> burnt. They tried to burn the roof of the church by
> piling up the chairs, like a bonfire."*

> *A pastor from Madugrui said: "Every day we carry new corpses to the cemetery. They kill farmers. They destroy our homes and churches. They kidnap and rape women."*
>
> *Ta'aziya from Karamai said: "We could see bullets whizzing. Everything was destroyed. In our whole village, only two of the homes were not burnt. Almost 50 people were killed."*
>
> *As a final example, it was my agonising privilege to weep with and to hug Veronica, from Dogon Noma, who told me: "They attacked me with a machete twice, once to the neck and once to my hand." I saw the scars. She said: "They said they wanted my daughter to suck my finger. So they amputated my forefinger and I passed out. When I woke up, I saw my six year-old daughter on the ground, dead, with my chopped finger in her mouth."*

In February 2020 Caroline was appointed Co-Chair of the All-Party Parliamentary Group (APPG) on International Freedom of Belief, and in June 2020, the APPG released its important and authoritative report: "Nigeria: Unfolding Genocide?" The report received fair and widespread media coverage in *The Times*, *The Independent*, *The Telegraph*, on BBC News, and elsewhere. It also sent shockwaves through Nigeria. President Buhari himself was forced to issue a statement. Yet despite his assurances, nothing appears to have changed.

On 15 June 2020, Baroness Cox wrote in the "Comment" section of *The Telegraph*.

> Just a few weeks ago, the UK joined the world in commemorating the 26th anniversary of

the Rwandan genocide, when in 1994, at least 800,000 Rwandans were murdered.

Every year, we lay wreaths to remember the personal tragedies and to mark the horrific scale of the killing. We remember the victims, survivors and all those who risked their lives to stop the horror. And every year, we say "never again" – never again will we fail to act, nor turn our back on those who suffer such unspeakable violence. Never again will we stand aside as perpetrators of atrocities commit their crimes with impunity. Ominously, however, history can very easily be repeated.

In Nigeria's northern and central belt states, thousands of civilians have been killed in attacks led by Boko Haram, Islamist Fulani herders and other extremist militias. Hundreds of churches have been burned to rubble. Entire communities have been forced to abandon their homes and farmland.

I have had the painful privilege of visiting some of the worst affected areas... In every village, the message from local people is the same: "Please, please help us! We are not safe in our own homes." Yet time and again, the world appears to ignore their cry for help.

I, and many colleagues in Parliament, have frequently sought to raise their concerns by meetings with ministers, evidence to inquiries, letters, formal questions and debates – and today, by the publication of a new report by the All-Party Parliamentary Group for Freedom of

Religion or Belief, entitled "[Nigeria:] Unfolding Genocide?" which details the horrific killing of innocent civilians.

To date, the UK Government's response has been woefully inadequate. It insists the "situation" in Nigeria has little to do with religion or ideology. They refer to the Islamist insurgency as "a consequence of population growth", "land and water disputes" or "tit-for-tat clashes between farmers and herders". Even as militant groups such as Boko Haram and ISWAP sweep across the Sahel, imposing their extremist ideologies with violence on those who refuse to comply, the UK continues to underplay the scale of massacres or that a genocide may be occurring.

Such an inappropriate response by our Government is an insult to those who are suffering so much. The causes of violence are, of course, complex. But given the escalation, frequency, organisation, brutality and asymmetry of attacks against predominantly Christian communities, is it not time to give greater effect to our obligations as a signatory to the 1948 Genocide Convention and our duty to protect?

There is no place here for moral equivalence. Nor is it sufficient for our Government merely to "emphasise the importance of mediation and inter-faith dialogue" – important though these may be. For the longer we tolerate these massacres and atrocities, the more we embolden the perpetrators. We give them a "green light"

to fulfil their reign of terror and to carry on their
killing and destruction with impunity.

Two voices for Nigeria's voiceless

For decades, acting both as a concerned Christian believer
and a British parliamentarian, Baroness Cox has released
gripping and precise eyewitness reports and analyses about the
impending genocide in Nigeria. And her steadfast friend and
ally Archbishop Ben Kwashi has continued to provide her with
trustworthy reports from the ground, documenting the plight of
his people.

As years have passed, no Nigerian has offered a more
endearing and truthful "voice for the voiceless" as Archbishop
Benjamin Kwashi. As we've seen, no faith leader has personally
faced greater injury and continuous danger than that which he
and his family have endured. And no one in Nigeria has summed
up the present desperation of his country's Christian believers,
churches, and communities with such eloquence and honesty –
although some of the hard truths are uncomfortable reading for
a Western audience. While battling health concerns of his own,
he recently said:

> In northern Nigeria, if you are a Muslim and
> you kill a Christian, you're most likely to go
> free. You can get away with murder – literally.
> There is a culture of impunity in Nigeria, and the
> government is either powerless or lacks the will
> to prevent the killing.
>
> If you see the kinds of people that are being
> killed, no sane human being would accept that

climate change is causing violence. Children are slaughtered; literally, this is a killing of the poorest of the poor. They are being killed, and we're still making an excuse that this is because of climate change?

I believe that the current system of governance in Nigeria gives Christians no hope beyond their trust in God... When the government fails to protect its citizens, it is, in effect, licensing untrained vigilantes to carry out extrajudicial justice, while the lawmakers, the military, and the police look on. This is what has happened in Nigeria.

The effect of this is that children, old people, women, and unarmed civilians are being hacked to pieces in their beds. By refusing to restrain murderers, the government is forcing people to rise to defend themselves. The situation is getting worse.

But I have hope because of my faith in God

from '"Culture of impunity" over violence in Nigeria, says Archbishop of Jos' by Adam Becket, *The Church Times*, 19 July 2019.

To this day, Baroness Cox continues to share the heartfelt mission first presented to her by then Bishop Ben Kwashi. Decades ago he asked her, "Will you tell the world what is happening here in Nigeria?"

In the many years since, Baroness Cox has done precisely that.

Chapter Six

Sudan and South Sudan – Twin Quests for National Transformation

In the dry season, when towering clouds, drenching rains, and flash floods are but just a memory, parts of Sudan and South Sudan look very different from the air. From horizon to horizon, much of the South is a vast, flat savannah, with the shadows of former rivers etched into the cracked soil. The terrain is harsh and empty. It was once the domain of lions, leopards, and gazelles before years of war and famine caused much that was alive to be devoured.

The two great nations have long been an arena for interaction between the diverse cultural and religious traditions of Muslim Arabs, Muslim and Christian non-Arabs, and animists. Tensions between – and within – North and South have continued for generations. Before South Sudan was declared a separate country in 2011, numerous groups engaged in conflict with each other for most of the years since gaining independence from Britain on 1 January 1956, when the Republic of Sudan was officially established.

By 1989, an Islamist military regime took power by coup, declaring war against all who opposed it. Two of their key objectives: the Islamisation of those who were not already Muslims; and the Arabisation of the African peoples. Resistance to the regime embroiled Sudan in a protracted and bitter conflict, in which 2 million perished and 4 million were displaced. Even now – as we will see through Baroness Cox's eyes – conflict continues.

The Sudanese People's Liberation Army (SPLA), led by the US-educated and Fort Benning-trained Colonel John Garang de Mabior, held its ground for two decades until peace talks during 2002 to 2004 led to a peace treaty being signed in January 2005. This treaty gave autonomy to Southern Sudan for six years, to be followed by a referendum for independence. John Garang was sworn in as Sudan's vice president on 9 July 2005, second only to his long-time adversary President Omar Al-Bashir.

Garang and Bashir began to forge a power-sharing government between the North and the South, which would elevate Garang's SPLA to a status equal to that of Bashir's Sudanese military. However, John Garang died in a helicopter crash while returning from Uganda to Southern Sudan just three weeks after being sworn into office. Many believe his demise was no accident.

Meanwhile, the conflict in Darfur, Sudan, which flared up in 2003, had displaced another 2 million Sudanese and cost 400,000 more people their lives. The only good thing that can be said for the Darfur crisis is that it finally turned the world's eyes towards Sudan's agony.

Along with other largely ignored human rights advocates, Baroness Cox was hard at work in Sudan long before the Darfur tragedy became headline news. By that time, she had embarked on dozens of dangerous, illicit missions to pre-Independent Southern Sudan, the Nuba Mountains, the Southern Blue Nile, and the eastern lands inhabited by the Beja people. She also made one official visit to the Sudanese capital, Khartoum, to hear the regime's version of events. These early beginnings of focused concern paved the way for Lady Cox's ongoing work in Sudan and South Sudan, which continues today.

But, like much else in her remarkable life, her first introduction to that troubled country took a rather unlikely turn.

An unexpected adventure

It was 1985 and Caroline's second son, Jonathan, was working as a nurse in Sudan with an excellent mission organisation named Emmanuel International (known as Fellowship for African Relief, as Christian titles were forbidden). After a few months, he sent an urgent request to London for either Caroline's daughter, Pippa, or her daughter-in-law, Poppy, to come and help – there was a crippling shortage of nurses. Neither young woman was able to go. Although by that time she was already "Baroness Cox", since she was a nurse herself, Caroline impulsively asked Jonathan if perhaps she could be of some help. He was so astounded that he sent back a very enigmatic message "What a concept!"

After hastily making arrangements, Caroline arrived in Khartoum, and EI promptly sent her to work with a Canadian nurse, Kathryn, in Northern Kordofan. The two women were tasked with introducing an immunisation programme into that very remote part of Sudan where there was no vaccine protection for TB, polio, tetanus, diphtheria, typhoid, or measles.

In order to begin their work in far-flung locations, Caroline and Kathryn had to pay personal visits to the local sheikhs or chieftans to obtain their permission and cooperation. The sheikh in one village was especially grateful when they visited him – two of his sons had recently died of measles.

On another occasion Caroline and Kathryn needed to call on a distant village, and they headed out in an old Land Rover. The only directions they had were to drive towards a distant mountain – their destination was supposedly nearby. But after driving through empty desert for about two hours, their vehicle came to an abrupt stop – and refused to move an inch further.

Stuck in the middle of nowhere, there was no option for the two nurses but to walk towards that far-off mountain, carrying their water bottles. As they trudged through sand so hot it burned their feet, they were beginning to think they would never reach their destination, and worse, that this was to be their end.

Suddenly, a boy's face appeared over the edge of a *wadi* (ravine), and he led them to a small cluster of huts where the local people welcomed them with great generosity: one moment, a little goat was licking Caroline's feet; minutes later, they were offered the freshest goat meat they had ever tasted.

The local people also graciously provided them with a hut for the night. But Caroline found sleep difficult – she had no idea how they were going to get back to their starting point, Hamrat El-Wiz. First thing in the morning, she tentatively asked if there were any camels locally and whether it would be possible to be given a ride home. Although there was only one camel, the local people were, again, very generous and helpful. They saddled the animal as usual, then devised a second makeshift saddle fastened around the camel's neck.

Caroline gave Kathryn the proper saddle and climbed onto precarious perch in front of her. The camel turned his proud head around, took one look at the two nurses and decided he didn't approve, spitting green cud all over them. Of course, they were well aware that it was important not to fall off, so they hung on with all their might as the camel stood up and started the long journey, thankfully with his owner walking alongside.

Neither woman was dressed for camel riding, so the constant striding movement of the camel became uncomfortable. Also, the animal had a fetish for mega-cactus plants and when it spied one on the horizon, it would gallop ahead, leaving its owner far behind, while crunching on the toughest and sharpest vegetation imaginable.

After two hours, Caroline and Kathryn were relieved still to be on board and began talking to pass the time.

Two hours later, exhaustion and thirst began to set in, so they silently endured the constant, challenging pacing of the large animal.

Two more hours passed. After six hours on the camel's back, Caroline heard a faint voice from behind:

"Caroline, I think I'm going to faint. Please could you tell me some stories?"

Realising that if Kathryn were to faint and fall off the camel they would be in far worse circumstances, Caroline tried to swallow a few times and launched into relating every story she could think of. And at last, after about another hour, she caught sight of the sun shining on the corrugated iron roofs of the huts in Hamrat-El Wiz in the distance.

As they drew near, it occurred to Caroline that their arrival would be the strangest sight the people had ever seen. First of all, in that part of Sudan, women do not ride camels. To unexpectedly see these two female *khawajas* (a not very complimentary term for white people) riding on a camel would be a source of great hilarity. Before long, the village children would run towards them, point, laugh, and shout, followed by adults and, before long, the whole population of this little township would come out to share the joke.

With Kathryn feeling weak, Caroline felt she needed to offer some sage advice. She spoke over her shoulder, alerting her friend to the inevitable scenario that lay ahead and encouraged her to join in the fun – no matter how terrible she was feeling – with the words of the proverbial saying:

> Laugh and the world laughs with you.
> Weep and you weep alone.
> For this brave old earth has need of your mirth
> It has troubles enough of its own.

Encountering Al-Turabi and his regime

It is certainly true that Sudan has long had troubles enough of its own. And Lady Cox has seen, felt, and reported more than her share of them.

As early as December 1992, Lady Cox described the state of Sudan's abused population vividly in the House of Lords, and made a plea for Britain to honour its historic obligations to the Sudanese. "The people feel forgotten and betrayed by the rest of the world," she told her peers. "I hope that we in Britain will not fail them in their hour of need."

That debate in the House of Lords lasted two hours and twenty-seven minutes. And watching the proceedings from the gallery, with increasing discomfort, were the Sudanese ambassador and a handful of other Sudanese embassy representatives.

"If looks could kill," Caroline later recalled, "I most certainly would not be alive today."

After the debate, Cox was invited to the Sudanese embassy to hear about the many "good and praiseworthy things" that were being done by the Khartoum government. She gladly agreed to the embassy meeting, but as it dragged on she managed to interrupt what she later described as a monologue of self-congratulation, and she invited herself to Sudan. She wanted to see for herself if what was being said was true.

So, in July 1993, Caroline Cox flew into the capital of Sudan with a small team that included Adam Kelliher, a cameraman from Frontline News. Their first day in Khartoum coincided with an indoor gathering to mark the fourth anniversary of the military regime's coup and ascent to power. On the balcony at the rear of the Hall of Friendship, a group of mujahedin were shouting chants. A bearded, white-robed imam, brandishing a great sword, led the assembled crowd in a rallying cry for holy war. All in attendance were urged to respond to the cry of the jihadis, to close ranks and reduce their country's fragmentation.

The spirit of jihad was also on parade at the Hussein Ben Ali Popular Defence Force training ground, where white-uniformed, Kalashnikov-carrying mujahedin marched up and down, chanting, "There is only one God and Mohammed is his prophet", and "We are soldiers of Allah." The crowd was reminded that those who gave their lives in the Holy War would become *shu'hada* – martyrs – assured by the Koran of being rewarded with innumerable sensual delights in Paradise.

"We noticed," Caroline wrote in her notes, "that the virtually compulsory militia requires all its members, be they Muslims, Christians or animists, to sing Islamic chants. The pledge of the government to intensify its programme of Islamisation is a cause of great concern to Sudan's non-Muslims."

A meeting was arranged with the leading figure of Sudan's National Islamic Front, Dr Hassan Al-Turabi, who courteously received the group in the wood-panelled reception room at his home. After they were settled into plush leather sofas and had been offered tea and cool drinks, Dr Al-Turabi, the Speaker of the Sudanese Parliament, began a monologue. A slight figure behind black-rimmed glasses and a close-cropped grizzled white beard, he spoke at length, using his hands for emphasis, and smiling reassuringly. But the meeting was less than convivial. "He just opened his mouth and out flowed non-stop propaganda," Caroline Cox noted.

Her anger mounting, she began to challenge his assertions. She suspected that many of his visitors would be unfamiliar with the complexities of the situation in Sudan and might accept his propaganda unquestioningly. The more he persisted, the more she interrupted, challenging the untruths in his spiel. Dr Al-Turabi did not find the novelty amusing; the smile vanished, and his face grew darker as the atmosphere chilled. When it dawned on Dr Al-Turabi that this exchange was being filmed, he became angrier still, and he abruptly terminated the interview. All courtesies were suspended as Cox and her colleagues were unceremoniously ushered out of his house.

Sudan's notorious "peace camps"

On that same journey, Caroline Cox visited refugee camps in the North and the Nuba Mountains, a range some 300 miles south of El-Obeid, rising 1,370 metres above the surrounding plains. The mountains are inhabited by people from the Nuba tribes, many of whom were being held in refugee centres that bore a striking resemblance to concentration camps.

Conditions in the camps were appalling. An atmosphere of lethargy and demoralisation was pervasive. The people Cox interviewed reported that they had been forced into the camps after government troops had attacked their homes and villages, burned their houses and crops, destroyed their waterholes, and left them with nothing. Short of death by thirst or starvation, their only option was the so-called "Peace Camps".

Foreign non-governmental organisations (NGOs) were denied access to the camps, and a propaganda campaign had been launched by Khartoum against the NGOs. With a ban on humanitarian missions, Western relief aid could be distributed only by Islamic organisations, which had sole rights to operate in the camps. In Khartoum, churches were permitted a small share in the distribution of aid, but in the Nuba Mountains camps, and elsewhere in the South, rations were distributed only to those who were willing to convert to Islam. To obtain food and medicine, many of the displaced said they were ordered to renounce their Christian names and adopt Islamic ones. Caroline called it "the politics of hunger".

She later recalled how, on several occasions, she encountered people starving and dying of treatable diseases, who could have gone to Government of Sudan health clinics or feeding centres but refused to do so. Conversion to Islam was the price tag on food and water. These malnourished, thirsty people asserted that they were Christians and would prefer to die as Christians rather than convert to Islam in order to obtain life-saving food and medicine.

One picture remains etched on Caroline Cox's heart: a young, blind, virtually naked mother holding a starved infant. The mother explained that she would not go to a government clinic or feeding centre, as she would not convert to Islam. Caroline Cox later reflected, "It would be a tough call to sacrifice one's own life for one's faith. To sacrifice your child must be the ultimate anguish – but that is the price people were prepared to pay on the front line of faith in Sudan."

Cox's visits to Sudan continued over the next few months, all conducted without official permission and all involving illegal entry into areas of the country designated "no-fly zones" by the Khartoum regime. It was their policy to carry out military offensives against innocent civilians while simultaneously closing those combat zones to the United Nations-led Operation Lifeline Sudan and all the major aid organisations working under the UN umbrella. Consequently, no one could provide aid for the government's victims, or witness the atrocities it was perpetrating, or tell the world what it was doing. It was in these areas that Caroline Cox and her colleagues saw the raw and ruthless brutality of Khartoum's National Islamic Front, a regime that was never elected but, until relatively recently, was recognised as the government of Sudan.

Wherever possible, Caroline Cox met leaders of the opposition groups, who, judging by the votes cast at the annulled election, represented some ninety per cent of the Sudanese people.

In 1994, the year that a new government offensive sent 100,000 Southern Sudanese refugees fleeing into Uganda, Lady Cox visited Dr John Garang. One of his principal disputes with the North concerned the introduction of Islamic law. He dismissed Dr Turabi's insistence that Shari'a law would not be applied to the South. "It is impossible to exempt the South from the supreme laws of the land," he explained to Baroness Cox. "The National Islamic Front will not accept a secular state; we will not accept an Islamic state."

By June 1994, the situation was deteriorating rapidly. Severe fighting had led to the evacuation of 80,000 from the relief camps. Most NGOs had been forced to quit, and the food lifeline was severed. In Mayen Abun, in the Bahr El-Ghazal region, people and cattle were starving. In the previous year, ninety per cent of the local crops had been destroyed by drought.

The rains had held off from July to April. Now the seed had shrivelled and blown away. Malnutrition was rife, along with malaria, TB, pneumonia, and diarrhoea. Even leprosy was making a comeback – and it was only the beginning of the hungry season. There were four months to go before harvest, and already most of the roots and grasses had been eaten.

A few yards from the airstrip where her small aircraft had landed, Caroline came across two of hunger's victims. A man of around fifty had walked for more than five days to find food, and had found nothing. Meanwhile, an eighteen-year-old girl lay in the shade of a thorn tree, dying of starvation and TB. Her skin was stretched tightly across her skull. She was beyond the capacity to digest food and there was no medicine for her. She had only hours to live. Caroline did what she could, taking the time to provide a drink of water, to say a quiet prayer with the two victims, to hold their hands and touch their foreheads, to somehow comfort them in their dying moments. They were so weak they could not lift their limbs, yet they responded with wide smiles of appreciation. The next morning, when Caroline returned to visit them, they were both dead.

That same day Lady Cox encountered Akel Deng, a young widow who was naked to her waist apart from a locket. Her husband had died an hour earlier. She knelt in silence on a mat of reeds beside the dead body, her face a mask of grief and resignation, her hands lifted to God. For half an hour, Caroline knelt alongside Akel, her arm embracing the bereaved woman. Sharing grief across a vast cultural divide, the two quietly cried and prayed together.

Later on, Akel's husband was laid to rest in the red soil. Akel tried to comfort one wailing child while another hid behind a tree, unable to face what had happened to his father. "My heart broke over the extent of the suffering and for the fact that so much of it is forgotten," Cox later said. "The rest of the world doesn't know and doesn't seem to care."

Father Benjamin Madol Akot, a Roman Catholic priest, thanked Caroline for choosing to open her eyes to their need. "We have felt deserted, even betrayed, by Christians in the West. We have suffered for twenty-seven years, seeking help, but it doesn't materialise."

If possible, things were even worse in the Nuba Mountains. There were some 3 million Nuba, from a variety of tribes. These were black Africans, most of whom spoke Arabic as their first language. Some forty per cent were Muslim; up to thirty per cent were Christian, and the rest were animist. Yet Muslims, Christians, and animists alike were being systematically ousted from their homes by government forces. Around a quarter of a million were living in territory nominally under SPLA control while many more had been displaced.

The church in the Nuba Mountains had been cut off from the outside world for more than a decade, though their problems had begun even earlier, in 1962, when the military regime of General Abboud had expelled all missionaries from the country. There were few clergy, yet the church had continued to thrive, kept alive by a few priests and the dedicated, courageous catechists. They made up for their lack of education with zeal, braving snake and insect bites and malaria to travel around the country performing their Christian duties.

The Nuba Anglican priests had nothing, so Caroline Cox and her team gave them Bibles and service books, and even handed over their own wristwatches. In return, the hungry priests gave them a hen, which Caroline entrusted back to them with a smile, promising to return to share a meal of freshly laid eggs at some later date.

"You are the first Christians who have come to encourage us," said Benjamin Barnaba, the Anglican co-director of the Nuba New Sudan Council of Churches. "We will never forget you."

A town called Nyamlell

During the mid-1990s, Caroline got to know Sudan rather well. But nothing had prepared her for what she was to find in Nyamlell, located in today's South Sudan. Adjacent to the town was an airstrip that the government had closed to aid deliveries. As usual, all entry was forbidden to NGOs. Caroline and her team ignored the prohibition and no sooner had their Cessna Caravan touched down on the landing strip, whipping up clouds of dust, than people appeared from all directions to greet them, relief written large on their faces.

"Thank God you've come!" announced Commissioner Aleu Akechak Jok, a clean-shaven, bespectacled man in Western clothes. He was a judge who had given up his practice in Khartoum to be with his people in their war. "We thought the world had completely forgotten us."

Nyamlell had not recovered from a brutal attack by jihadi warriors in March 1995, two months before. Encouraged and equipped by the government of Khartoum, some 2,000 well-armed men had descended on the village on horseback. They were Arabs from the Rizeigat and Misseriya tribes, along with Government of Sudan Army soldiers and members of the Popular Defence Forces (PDF). They killed eighty-two villagers, mainly men, and wounded many more, leaving the old for dead. They torched houses, seized livestock, stripped the village of every personal possession – even cooking pots – and rounded up the cattle. Herded behind the horses, with the cattle, were

282 women and children. Nyamlell's airstrip was one of those closed by Khartoum. Not only did this prevent outside aid from reaching the villagers, but, again, it kept outsiders' eyes from seeing what had happened.

By the time Caroline Cox arrived, eight weeks had passed since the militia's assault. In the blackened ruins of their *tukuls* (homes), remaining townsfolk lined up to bear witness. Others emerged from the bush, having walked for hours to describe similar attacks on their own villages. "We were armed with spears and they were armed with Kalashnikovs," reported Garang Amok Mou, who had lost seven brothers – four killed and three captured. "My brothers were killed because they were holding spears to try to rescue their families, and they were mown down by gunfire. We cannot possibly defend our people when we only have traditional weapons to fight against well-armed militias with automatic rifles."

Abuk Marou Keer is blind. She appeared one afternoon wearing a tattered grey top over a pastel-coloured skirt. She described how she had been hauled to her feet and almost strangled by her beads. She and her children were taken away with the other captives, beaten, then forced to walk. She stumbled sightlessly behind the horses, struggling to carry property that had not been looted by her captors. Their destination was an agricultural labour camp at Araith, eighteen miles to the north. "Four male captives were murdered by the Arabs," she explained to Caroline Cox, "and many women were raped." She was among them:

> The soldiers said this was retaliation for the death of one of their leaders in the raid against Nyamlell... we were also forced to grind grain from sunrise to sunset. All we had to eat was the leftover waste

from grinding. We were beaten, sometimes with
whips, but they left our hands untied.

Abuk Keer tried her best to describe the desperation she felt. Because of her blindness, she had been abandoned when her two children were taken away as slaves. She quietly explained:

In Africa, if you are blind, your children are your
eyes. I am blind; I have lost my children. I will
die. I have been told by Arab traders that my
children are alive and they know where they are.
But they need money to buy their freedom –
and I don't have any money or anything left
after this raid.

Caroline Cox and her colleagues risked providing the money Abuk needed to pay Arab traders the price of her children's freedom. When they returned to Nyamllel a few months later, a very happy Abuk Keer was sitting in her home with a radiant smile, exclaiming, "I am so happy my children have come home! If I weren't blind, I could dance all night. We are together as a family. That is all that matters."

Slave-traders in the modern world

It was in Nyamlell that Baroness Cox first became an eyewitness to the trading of slaves. There she heard testimony after testimony about women and children who had been herded behind horses after a raid, taken captive to be sold into slavery. Many ended up in Northern Sudan, but others were transported to homes or armies in the Middle East and even Europe.

In his 1995 report "Situation of Human Rights in the Sudan", United Nations Special Rapporteur of the Commission of Human Rights, Gáspár Bíró, wrote of an "alarming increase in the number of reports" from a wide variety of sources of cases of slavery in Sudan. He wrote of an incident in Aweil,

> … where PDF troops… took thousands of cattle and abducted some 500 women and 150 children between five and twelve years of age… taken to Al-Islamiyya, an Islamic non-governmental organization active in the field of education, while the government claims that they are displaced children. Big boys are distributed as workers… they work in the fields or as servants… Girls become concubines or wives, mainly of soldiers and PDF members in Northern Sudan… Dinka boys as young as 11 or 12 years reportedly receive military training and are sent by the government of Sudan to fight the war in Southern Sudan… The Special Rapporteur cannot but conclude that the… traffic in and sale of children and women, slavery, servitude, forced labour and similar practices are taking place with the knowledge of the government of Sudan… The manifest passivity of the government of Sudan… after years of reporting… leads to the conclusion that abductions, slavery and institutions and practices similar to slavery are carried out by persons acting under the authority and with the tacit approval of the government of Sudan.

Gaspar Biro was later banned from Sudan. At around the same time, Caroline Cox stepped into the nightmare herself, and defiantly made illicit trips to Nyamlell and other destinations with foreign media correspondents in tow, meeting slave traders, redeeming hundreds of Sudanese slaves, setting them free, and making sure every transaction was recorded on videotape for all the world to see.

Two decades later, during a remarkable and unexpected encounter in Abyei, a young man called Arop Dombek Deng approached Caroline to ask if she was "Lady Cox". With a beaming smile, he told her: "You saved me. Twenty years ago. You negotiated my freedom. You saved my life. All the other children remember the name 'Lady Cox'. It's because of you I am here."

Such redemptions, however, were a controversial effort. And Cox did not look upon it lightly. She later described her reaction to the atrocity of slave trading:

> *The feelings are so deep and so complicated; it's hard to verbalise them. Immense, deep grief. If you talk to a mother whose children are currently slaves, what do you say? There aren't any words to describe it. Deep anger. And this is part of a systematic policy, being pursued and encouraged by a government that is sitting in Khartoum. It makes me feel intense anger and a passionate commitment to try to do something about it, to try and expose it, to try to get it stopped, to try to free anyone who I could.*

Baroness Cox continues to defend her policy by pointing out that those who criticise slave redemption do not understand the situation.

This slavery is not economic. It is a weapon of war. This enslavement would take place on this massive scale, whether or not we ever redeemed a single slave. And we believe there is a moral mandate to set the slave free. Let those who criticise criticise us in London, Nairobi or New York come and see the reality – and then they will be in a position to judge for themselves if they could leave women and children in slavery with a clear conscience.

The quest for a safe and strong South Sudan

After generations of turmoil, a 2005 Comprehensive Peace Agreement (CPA) led to the establishment of a Government of National Unity – an entity designed to bring together previously warring factions in Sudan's North and South. However, the CPA created many problems for the South. It did not provide fair and effective representation in key government positions for Southerners, nor did it assure justice in the distribution of Sudan's potentially abundant natural resources, particularly in the sharing of oil revenues.

In 2006, Caroline Cox chose to lead a team into Yei because that town epitomised so many of the problems. Yei had been the focus of intense battles as it changed hands repeatedly between the NIF (National Islamic Front) and the SPLA (Sudan People's Liberation Army). For several years it had also sustained such repeated and heavy bombardment that it was largely devastated. Bishop Elias Taban and other community leaders met Caroline Cox and her colleagues and accompanied them to an orphanage, a clinic, a hospital under construction, and a college that provides teacher training and theological education. "We were deeply touched by the love, warmth and standard of care at the orphanage," Lady Cox declared.

> *The nurses at the clinic were also impressive in*
> *their professional competence. We discussed with*
> *them the urgent need for more community nurses*
> *and midwives to provide clinical care in outlying*
> *areas. As the clinic serves a large catchment area*
> *with a diameter of approximately 50 miles, many in*
> *need of treatment may be unable to obtain it. Some*
> *treatment could usefully be provided by mobile*
> *medical units, but there is also a great need for*
> *more preventive healthcare and health education,*
> *especially in the more remote areas.*

During that 2006 visit to Sudan, Baroness Cox also heard expressions of deep concern over the rapid increase in Islamic aid organisations – a concern because some leaders feared that such organisations would cynically use the humanitarian crisis in Sudan to introduce the militant Wahhabist form of Islam. And in fact, in February 2006, President Al-Bashir proclaimed the government's intention to pour money into the South for humanitarian purposes. His promise was welcomed by some, but others saw it as part of an Islamic agenda. They expressed concern that Islamic NGOs often used relief supplies as a means to promote conversion to Islam. "Such a conversion," one leader said, shaking his head, "is a one-way street."

It was well known that once people agreed to become Muslim – even if they do so only as a means of getting food, water, medical care, or other necessities – it is difficult and dangerous to "un-convert". Under some interpretations of

Shari'a law, such recanting is considered "apostasy", an offence that carries with it, at best, the likelihood of rejection by family and friends, but also the very real possibility of the death penalty. One community leader said, "The NIF will achieve its Islamist agenda through winning in peace what it failed to achieve by war."

Across the years, Caroline Cox visited Sudan during the war that was first unleashed by President Al-Bashir and his regime. She wept with the people as she walked through the killing fields with hundreds of corpses and the burnt-out villages in every state from Bahr-El-Ghazal in the West, Yei and Nimule in the South, the Equatorias and Upper Blue Nile in the East.

On many visits, she accompanied the widely renowned Catholic bishop Macram Gassis. She recalls, "I will never forget his preaching in a village where every building, including the church had been destroyed and the people met for worship under the branches of a tamarind tree. His words express my feelings then and now, but far more eloquently."

Bishop Gassis poured out encouragement on his people,

Here we are, in this beautiful cathedral, not made by human hands but by nature and by God – and it is filled with the people of God and especially with children. You people in Sudan still smile, in spite of suffering, persecution and slavery. Your smiles put us to shame. Many of you are naked and embarrassed by your nakedness. Don't be embarrassed. Yours is not true nakedness. True nakedness is to be without love. Therefore, be clothed in love – that is true Christianity – and show your love to those who do not know our Lord of Love. Do not think we will forget you. You

will be remembered as those who are closest to
God because every day you are obeying Christ's
command to take up His cross and to follow Him.
We will pray for you – but prayer without deeds is
dead. Our prayer and our love must be in action
for you. I came, I saw, I heard, I touched – and I
am enriched.

The painful birth of a new country

On 9 July 2011 – after decades of bloodshed, political upheaval,
and violent conflict – South Sudan officially raised its colorful
flag of red, green, white, black, blue, and a yellow star, heralding
its independence. It had become Africa's fifty-fourth country,
with its capital in Juba. Lady Cox was honoured by an invitation
to the fledgling state's Independence Day celebrations. It was a
joyful and festive event, and its elation and optimism lingered
for a while.

During the formalities, the occasion felt like the beginning
of a new era – the peaceful resolution of a long, wearying expanse
of death and destruction. South Sudanese citizens swarmed
the capital of Juba by the thousands to celebrate the country's
birth, while Sudanese People's Liberation Army (SPLA) soldiers
marched proudly, their AK-47 rifles in hand.

Hopes soared that day that the newly born country of South
Sudan could finally celebrate peace and be removed by a firm
border from the North's brutality. But, sadly, the bloodshed
was far from over. Less than three years after South Sudan's
Independence Day, its own civil war began in December 2013.
It was triggered by a political dispute between President Salva
Kiir's SPLA and the opposition force led by former vice president,

Riek Machar. Rebel groups have since proliferated along ethnic or tribal lines, forming localised militias, attacking civilian populations, and causing further disruption, devastation, and mass displacement.

On numerous occasions between 2014 and 2019 the warring parties committed themselves to forming a Transitional Government of National Unity. But ceasefire agreements were broken again and again, while the fighting continued. By 2020, they committed themselves once again to forming a Revitalised Transitional Government of National Unity, demonstrating a healthy spirit of compromise and political will. It is hoped this will lay the foundations for the next steps of the country's peace process and political transition, although sporadic violence between armed groups continues.

Baroness Cox persisted in visiting the people enduring these dangerous situations – both in Sudan and South Sudan. She wanted to hear the people's stories and to relate them, and to provide the urgently needed medical and food supplies they could not procure for themselves.

In January 2017, she found herself scaling a steep trail – a two-and-a-half hour trek in scorching heat. Her destination was a mountaintop in Dunou, where several hundred families had fled, seeking shelter in caves for fear of aerial bombardment. They were so desperate that they had remained there – despite the presence of deadly snakes. Those who lived in the caves regularly had to undertake that same exhausting climb to carry food and water. There was no healthcare available. One young girl Caroline spoke to had been bitten by a cobra and she had somehow managed to survive after being treated with traditional medicines.

Caroline entered one of the caves where she found a family crowded into an unbelievably cramped space in which they were unable to stand up. One woman was lying on a makeshift bed, seriously ill with malaria. No treatment was available. Nearby sat a despairing man who had lost five of his children – his sons and daughters had been burnt alive when a shell exploded, igniting a straw extension to the cave which he had built in an effort to provide a little more living space. He was left with just one little boy.

Shelling continued while the Baroness was there, and she later described that experience during testimony in the House of Lords.

> First, please travel with me in imagination to Sudan's Nuba mountains this January and climb a rugged mountain for two hours to meet families hiding in caves for fear of aerial bombardment. There we meet people suffering snake bites and dying from malaria with no medicine. Yet their priority for help is education, especially for girls. Schools are deliberately targeted by Government of Sudan bombers, so education and exams have to take place out of doors, using the respected Kenya curriculum. When it is time for exams, 1,000 students converge and invigilation is undertaken on the mountainside.
>
> Our valiant partner, Nagwa, asks every student to bring a large stone. As they gather, she tells them, "When you hear the Antonov bombers approaching while you are doing your exam, you will place your exam papers neatly under your large stone. You will then run and hide in the caves. When the bombers have gone, you can return. Your exam papers will not have been blown away by the blast or the wind and you can continue your exams." That is exam

pressure with a difference, and many of those students perform as well as their counterparts in Kenya.

Hansard, 9 March 2017, vol. 779, col. 1543

She went on to describe other tragedies further south:

I have had the privilege of visiting South Sudan more than 30 times, many during the previous war when 2 million people perished, 4 million were displaced and tens of thousands of women and children were abducted into slavery. Many are still missing and their families continue to grieve. But the people there still yearn for education as a priority. The Anglican bishop, Moses Deng, of the Diocese of Wau in Bahr El Ghazal, recognises the importance of education, especially for girls. He has supported the establishment of a school delightfully called "A Girls' School Which Boys May Attend". The girls do attend, and so do the boys, and their achievements are amazing. They attain some of the best results in the country.

Hansard, 9 March 2017, vol. 779, col. 1544

During that same visit in 2017, Lady Cox accompanied a woman named Mende Nazar to a very poignant reunion with her people and her homeland. In 1994, Mende had been captured and abducted into slavery from Karko – her village in the Nuba Mountains. This courageous woman had endured the horror of slavery for several years before being transported to

London in 2000 to work with a Sudanese diplomat's family. It was from there that she finally had escaped. She returned home to her people, where she was gathering evidence documenting the suffering inflicted by the regime through their policy of mass enslavement in South Sudan and the "Two Areas" of South Kordofan and Blue Nile states.

In the course of another visit to Blue Nile state in January 2018, Caroline went into a displaced persons' camp that had not been visited by any other NGO.

> *In Wadaka, the situation is extremely dire, with 9,000 IDPs who had recently fled from military offensives in Danfona in the middle of the night. They left carrying nothing with them and no help has reached them from any NGO. They said that HART was the first NGO to reach them. They are trying to survive, scavenging for food, eating leaves and roots with no nutritional value, to ease hunger pains. They have no other supplies such as clean water or blankets.*

One survivor told Caroline, "We lost everything. On the journey, some people were injured. They took all our cattle. We fled without anything. When we came here, there was nobody to help us."

Antar Juma, the chief of the JumJum tribe, pleaded for help from the humanitarian agencies in the international community: "I urge the humanitarian actors and agencies to find a way to help the people here in Wadaka because their needs are urgent and they're living in a very difficult situation. If no aid comes there will be more casualties. If this situation continues until next March there will be no people here." The people were desperate, eating roots and boiling leaves with no nutritional value to ease the pains of hunger. HART responded by initiating an emergency appeal, which raised £50,000 for sorghum (the common grain) and cooking oil.

"Your help has saved many lives," said Benjamin Kuku, from the New Sudan Council of Churches, who organised the safe and secure delivery of the food aid. "You [HART supporters] have shown love and mercy to the forgotten, marginalised and persecuted... Your compassion has been shared among the most vulnerable and they will remember you and we will remember this historical juncture of our struggle for survival forever."

Such life-saving assistance enabled families to survive for three months until the rainy season came. HART continues its advocacy to raise awareness of IDPs – in and beyond Blue Nile – and seeks to generate more aid for these neglected and suffering people.

The end of Omar al-Bashir and Sudan's new beginning

In 2018, as South Sudan struggled with its seemingly endless civil war, in the north, Sudan was experiencing escalating protests against the Khartoum regime. Demonstrators came from all levels of Sudanese society. They were united by one demand: the resignation of the infamous President, Omar al-Bashir, along with key members of his government. Unsurprisingly, Bashir's forces responded to the protests with lethal violence, shooting dead at least fifty-one between December 2018 and January 2019. They beat and locked up hundreds more. In February 2019, international news outlets reported "shocking footage" of security forces chasing protestors into a hospital, then opening fire.

But the fiery protection of Sudan's genocidal dictator was – at long last – unsuccessful. Omar Al-Bashir was overthrown by a group of top generals on 11 April 2019. He was arrested and reportedly transferred to a "maximum security prison" in Khartoum. He remains indicted by the International Criminal Court for war crimes and crimes against humanity, although Sudan's military said it will not extradite him and will try him in the country instead.

On 17 August 2019, the Transitional Military Council (TMC) and civilian leaders signed a deal as part of a planned 39-month transition to democracy. Watching from afar, Baroness Cox described her sense of guarded hopefulness.

The Sudanese people have experienced near-constant
conflict and instability over six decades of independence.
But I am cautiously optimistic that this Constitutional
Declaration will lead to the formation of a government
that can guarantee peace and stability throughout
Sudan. However, I share widespread concerns about
whether military and political officials associated with
the former regime will prove trustworthy partners –
especially given their history of repression and violence.
Clearly, the UK and its partners must maintain pressure
on the country's interim government and continue to
demand a clear timeline for a sustainable transition to
democracy. Real change must occur!

Abyei: massacre in Kolom

On Wednesday 22 January 2020, just after 7 a.m., nomadic Misseriya herders attacked the Dinka village of Kolom in the disputed Abyei area, which lies along the border between Sudan and South Sudan and is claimed by both countries. Herders arrived on tuk-tuks and motorbikes, armed with assault rifles and two RPG-7s. They killed thirty-two villagers and abducted fifteen children, aged between two and twelve. They also burned twenty-two *tukuls* and destroyed the local church and clinic.

Caroline visited the village just after the attack. "Many homes were still burning as we witnessed the digging of mass graves for the charred and mutilated bodies," she wrote to her HART supporters. "Survivors told us that, prior to the attack, they wanted to flee to the bush for safety. Yet they were urged by UNISFA (the United Nations Interim Security Force for Abyei), which is mandated to protect the local people, not to take this course of action." Several survivors described their frustration and despair to Baroness Cox:

> Six of our elders spoke with the UN on Tuesday night to warn them about an imminent attack by the Arab militants. The next day, all six of the elders were killed. Why didn't the UN protect us?
>
> We feared an attack at any moment, so we asked the local UN peacekeepers whether we should hide in the bush. But they told us not to worry and to stay in our homes. The UN left at 6.10 a.m. and the attack happened an hour later. The peacekeepers failed to protect us.
>
> If the UN will not protect us, then we must defend ourselves. Perpetrators must be brought to justice, otherwise there is a risk of retaliation. We are full of fear that there will be more violence and more deaths.

These survivors told Baroness Cox that the perpetrators were supported by the military regime in Khartoum, which reportedly provides arms in order to drive the indigenous Dinka people off their land – a tension that is exacerbated by the presence of oil in the region. This view was echoed by Kuol Alor, the chief administrator for Abyei, who told a reporter for *Middle East Eye*, "Definitely, the militia are backed by Khartoum." He said the attack was the "worst atrocity I have seen" and "the intention is to burn the villages so people can be driven out."

Another survivor told Caroline: "There have been other similar attacks [by Misseriya herders against civilian farmers] but this massacre was on a far greater scale. It is horrific. We are heartbroken. They burn our homes to occupy our land. We have never known anything like it."

The crisis facing civilians in Abyei is already complex and delicate. The local population has experienced years of severe suffering caused by armed conflicts, political challenges and devastating floods. There is deep concern that the horrors inflicted upon the villagers in Kolom may have far-reaching repercussions, aggravating tensions at this critical time for Sudan and South Sudan and threatening to spiral out of control.

Friendships forged in the heat of battle

Based on such dramatic episodes, it is clear that the countries of Sudan and South Sudan remain the source of both hopes for bright future peace and deep fears for the safety and wellbeing of the long-suffering Sudanese people. And yet, as is so often the case in intense conflict zones, deep friendships and powerful spiritual bonds are forged in the very heat of battle.

For example, in March 2017, 5,000 internally displaced women, men, and children flocked into Wau's cathedral compound seeking refuge from local violence. Archbishop Moses Deng had to borrow money from local traders to buy food for these IDPs, as many were on the brink of death from starvation. He sent an urgent request to HART asking for emergency funds for life-saving food. HART, being a very small NGO, was able only to send £10,000. However, the archbishop was profoundly grateful, saying this would buy a lot of sorghum (a cultivated grain and everyday food source). And, thankfully, it would also prevent the archbishop from being arrested for his inability to repay loans to local traders.

Meanwhile, peacemaking was necessary not only in large-scale national conflicts, but locally as well. When those 5,000 IDPs flooded into the cathedral compound, they came from three different tribal groups, historically alienated by animosity and conflict. Wise leadership, led by Archbishop Deng, exerted robust peacekeeping skills in their compound. Rather than dividing the quarrelling factions, they grouped individuals from the three tribes together. Desperate civilians laid down their resentments, and side by side they befriended one another. Three months later, they left together for a new IDP camp at Hai Masna. Reconciliation had been achieved and long-term hostility left behind.

HART quickly organised another urgent appeal and raised £50,000 for more sorghum and cooking oil. HART partnered with local organisation, New Sudan Council of Churches (NSCC), whose director is another friend of Baroness Cox and HART, Benjamin Barnaba.

Mr Barnaba gratefully told Baroness Cox, "Your help has saved many lives, you have shown love and mercy to the forgotten, marginalised and persecuted people on the planet today; your compassion is been shared among the most vulnerable and they will remember you and we will remember this historical juncture of our struggle for survival forever."

Caroline said recently,

> *I have been deeply grieved again to witness the suffering inflicted by the civil war: the killings, abuse of women, the destruction, and people forced to flee from fighting as refugees or as internally displaced people.*
>
> *But I also have hope: the civil war was almost inevitable given the legacy of the previous war: the tinderbox of a devastated infrastructure; only a few kilometres of tarmac road; a desperate shortage of professional personnel (only eight qualified midwives for the whole country); two generations of children unable to receive education because of intensive aerial bombardment by the Khartoum regime; hunger; unemployment; historic tribal conflicts... the list goes on.*
>
> *Yet the situation – which could have degenerated into another Rwandan-style genocide – did not. And although suffering on a huge scale continues, needing massive help, there are many positive initiatives being undertaken by courageous, resourceful local people, especially the Churches, building schools and clinics and working tirelessly to promote reconciliation and healing.*
>
> *The Sudanese people have suffered far too much for far too long. But they are still there, working hard to build a brighter future. And*

> *despite their pain they still smile their famous*
> *courageous Sudanese smiles, which make me feel*
> *very humble.*

As we've seen, one of those courageous and resourceful people is Moses Deng, Archbishop of Wau. He recently penned a warm tribute to Baroness Cox, which captures not only her courage and dedication, but recounts her innumerable journeys into the dark turmoil of both Sudan and South Sudan, bearing the light of Christ's love along with much-needed practical assistance. With HART's help, his people continue to provide for their African brothers and sisters.

In 2021, the Most Revd Moses Deng Bol wrote,

> I have known Baroness Caroline Cox since the
> 1990s during the war of liberation when she used
> to travel in the area – now known as Northern
> Bahr el Ghazal Internal Province – where I was
> serving as a young clergyman. She and her
> colleagues were redeeming or buying back slaves
> through an anti-slavery Christian organisation,
> Christian Solidarity International.
>
> The slave-traders were known as *muraleen*,
> moving on horseback into villages and small towns,
> capturing men, women, boys, and girls to be used
> by the by the Arab fighters as slaves or sex slaves.
>
> Baroness Cox used to travel in the same
> villages and small towns in the border between
> Southern and Northern Sudan – locations which
> were frequently raided by the muraleen or
> bombed from Antonov aircraft by the Sudanese
> Government. Some of the small towns she

visited included Mayen Abun, Turalei and Wun-Rok in Twich County, Marial Baai and Nyamlel in Aweil West County, and Warawar, Wanyjok and Malualkon in Aweil East county, just to mention but a few.

Baroness Cox gave the people of Southern Sudan hope during their dark days of struggle for freedom and she is still doing that today in war-torn South Sudan. Even though she is not officially representing the British Government, whenever she visits these dangerous places she leaves an impression to the Southern Sudanese that the British Government loves and cares for them.

Since I began my work in 2009 as Bishop of the Wau Diocese, Baroness Cox has always been the first to respond whenever I've sent an appeal to friends for assistance in an emergency situation in my Diocese – such as Relief for over 5,000 Internally Displaced Persons who came to the Cathedral compound in 2017. Lady Cox always says, "I cannot do everything, but I must not do nothing." And she has continued to visit and encourage the people of South Sudan and the Nuba Mountains since the war broke again in South Sudan in 2013.

So I have known Baroness Cox as a woman of courage, love, and compassion for the poor and oppressed. I have also known her as a committed Christian who has dedicated her life to do the will of God through the power of the Holy Spirit. Her commitment to freedom and justice for the

poor and the oppressed reminds me of Jesus'
statement in Luke 4:18–19:

"The Spirit of the Lord is on me,
because he has anointed me
to proclaim good news to the poor.
He has sent me to proclaim freedom for the
  prisoners
and recovery of sight for the blind,
to set the oppressed free,
to proclaim the year of the Lord's favour."

It is my prayer and hope that the struggles for
freedom and justice by the people of South
Sudan and Sudan and the support of friends like
Baroness Cox will eventually bring lasting peace
and prosperity to the two nations.

Chapter Seven

Syria – A Land of Conflicts, Near and Far

The Middle East and North Africa are home to some of the world's most intriguing and storied destinations in the world. Sandstone-hued towns and villages. Soaring minarets towering above turquoise-tiled mosques. Brilliantly colourful bazaars offering everything from trinkets to the finest of ceramics, textiles, and historical artefacts. The region's photogenic beauty is also evident in traditional, tribal, and religious attire as well as in the warm smiles of merchants, restaurateurs, and passers-by.

From Casablanca to Beirut to Cairo, from Istanbul to Baghdad to Jerusalem, ancient tales and legends come to life, while traces of antiquity are effortlessly discovered in museums, libraries and historic monuments. And Syria was once no exception.

However, storytellers performing in such romantic settings aren't always able to recount happy endings. Alongside the region's magical folklore and fables there also have been countless conflicts, many of them fiercer and more bloodstained than most Westerners – apart from archaeologists, anthropologists, and scholars of ancient history – care to know.

And these conflicts haven't been limited to long-ago wars. Even at the time of this writing, fighting continues in several Middle East war zones. Most of these conflicts can be dated from the same starting point. Syria's horrifying civil war serves as a prime example.

From "Arab Spring" to Syria's winter

The so-called Arab Spring began in December 2010 on the streets of Sidi Bouzid, Tunisia. It was in that small town that a desperate young street vendor, Mohammed Bouazizi, set himself alight in protest of a cruel police action – they had confiscated his vegetable stand because of Bouazizi's failure to obtain a proper permit.

Bouazizi's dramatic self-immolation (he later died of his wounds) literally ignited the "Jasmine Revolution" in Tunisia. Street protests in Tunis eventually escalated, and ultimately drove president Zine El Abidine Ben Ali out of the country.

Inspired by this conflict, activists across the Middle East stirred up protests large and small – some far more influential than others. But three countries were gripped by anti-regime violence that erupted into full-scale civil wars: Libya, Yemen, and Syria.

It was Syria, and the endangered religious minorities there, that drew Baroness Cox into the fray.

The Syrian conflict began on 6 March 2011, when fifteen teenagers from Daraa were arrested for scribbling anti-regime graffiti on the wall of their school. According to locals, when the families and friends of the young men protested against their arrest and demanded their release, security forces opened fire on them, killing three people.

Daily protests continued and rage escalated; buildings were burned including one owned by a cousin of Syria's President Bashar al-Assad. On 25 April, the Syrian military launched a massive crackdown, which continued until 5 May. By June 2011, UN investigators reported that more than 240 protestors had been killed. Thus began the horrific Syrian Civil War. And it quickly spread like wildfire across the country.

Apart from his own loyal inner circle, Bashir Assad has never been a beloved character in the Middle East. Although he was far from the only brutal dictator in the region, he was widely viewed as such both by local victims and an array of international critics. And once the conflict began, and after several shockingly violent confrontations, it wasn't long before calls for military intervention – seeking Assad's removal from power – began to resound across the free world.

Questions about foreign policy

In August 2013, after two years of increasingly distressing observation, Baroness Cox raised concerns in Parliament about the harmful impact of British foreign policy on Syria. Her statements are recorded in Hansard.

> My Lords, I normally speak only on countries where I have on-the-ground experience, which is not the case with Syria. However, I feel compelled to convey concerns expressed by people for whom I have profound respect, currently living and working in Syria, witnessing and enduring the horrific situation there.

First, I refer to Damascus-based Gregorios III, Melkite Greek Catholic Church Patriarch of Antioch. Speaking to the very respected charity, Aid to the Church in Need, he argued that military intervention by the West against the Assad regime in Syria would be disastrous, stressing that, despite the ongoing conflict, reconciliation initiatives are still viable and should be the top priority. While condemning chemical weapon attacks, he highlights concerns about foreign fighters coming into Syria, he says:

"Many people are coming from outside Syria to fight in the country. These fighters are fueling fundamentalism and Islamism... and the problem is compounded by the flow of arms into the country... The extremists are wanting to fuel hatred between the Christians and Muslims... and, instead of calling for violence, international powers need to work for peace".

Of course, not peace at any price, but serious consideration of alternative measures, as emphasised by the noble Lord, Lord West, and other noble Lords, and in accordance with paragraph 4(ii) of the paper on the UK Government's legal position, which states that, "it must be objectively clear that there is no practicable alternative to the use of force if lives are to be saved."

The Patriarch, who last week narrowly escaped a bomb blast close to his home in Damascus, has described the threat of Western armed intervention as "a tragedy – for the whole country and the whole Middle East".

He highlights the implications for the suffering of Syrian civilians, including the 450,000 Christians now either displaced within the country or forced to flee as refugees abroad. Describing his country until recently as a "beacon of hope for Christianity in the Middle East", he highlights growing concern that Christianity is being eradicated from the very place Christ and his first disciples once knew as their own.

It must also be emphasised that it is not only Christians who are suffering from the violence. Many Muslim groups and communities are also being attacked and are living in constant fear.

For many years, despite a despotic regime, Syria ensured freedoms for diverse faith traditions and for women, which were enviable in comparison with its neighbours in the Middle East. There are real fears that any replacement regime, almost inevitably ruled or influenced by Islamists, will reduce Syria to the potentially irreversible destruction of religious freedoms and women's rights.

I therefore share the profound concerns about a military intervention that could unleash even more suffering. Bringing the perpetrators of crimes against humanity to justice must be the priority, not supporting, either directly or indirectly, militias that are also committing heinous and egregious violations of human rights. Adding to the number of hapless refugees and escalating the conflict seems to be neither rational nor productive. It will simply add to the totality of human misery, and certainly the first to suffer will be the minorities in Syria.

29 August 2013, vol. 747, cols. 1765–67

By the time Baroness Cox spoke her first words to Parliament on the subject, the Syrian Civil War had become increasingly lethal. During September 2013, when she expressed those concerns, a chemical warfare attack reportedly took place on the Ghouta area of Damascus. United Nations weapons inspectors said that about 300 people were killed, although they did not attribute responsibility.

By early 2014, radicalised and brutally violent Islamist groups had rushed into the conflict, leaving bloodied footprints behind their massacres. In June that same year, the Islamic State of Iraq and Syria (ISIS) declared its "caliphate" in territory stretching from Aleppo, Syria, to Diyala, Iraq. This turn of events led to airstrikes against ISIS by the United States and five Arab countries. Then, in 2015, Russia stepped in to carry out its own aerial attacks, principally against ISIS but also against some of the anti-Assad armed groups.

A controversial invitation

In 2016, after months of communication with distraught Syrian Christian, Muslim, and Yazidi leaders who were quite literally caught in the crossfire, Baroness Cox received an invitation to visit Syria. She was included in a pastoral group organised by Revd Dr Andrew Ashdown, comprised of experts in both Middle

East and interfaith relations, including the highly respected Rt Revd Michael Nazir-Ali.

Traditionally, religious minorities have experienced consideration from the Assad government due to the minority status of his own Alawite heritage. And it was representatives of several such minority groups that invited Baroness Cox to Syria. These included Bishop Armash Nalbandian, Armenian Archbishop of Damascus of the Armenian Apostolic Church; Bishop Antoine Audo, Archbishop of the Chaldean Catholic Church in Syria; Revd Harout Selimian, President of the Armenian Evangelical Church in Syria; and the (Sunni) Grand Mufti of Syria, Dr Ahmad Badreddin Hassoun.

Caroline Cox accepted the invitation, to see for herself the realities on the ground, to listen to a wide range of voices – which were not being heard outside Syria – and to meet religious leaders, representatives of diverse political parties (including the political opposition), local communities, and internally displaced people. The visit also included a meeting with President Bashar Assad himself. And that specific meeting, more than any other aspect of the trip, raised the ire of the British government and media. They interpreted her visit – and specifically the group's meeting with Assad – as providing legitimacy to his regime.

"This, clearly, is a misrepresentation of our position," Caroline said at the time. "I have never condoned violations of human rights by President Assad and his government. But as Cardinal Robin Eames said in a recent conference on Syria, 'If one is to move forward, one has to be prepared to shake hands with people with blood on them.' In promoting the peace process in Northern Ireland, Eames certainly did so."

When reflecting on the controversy later on, she recalled a pre-visit meeting with Bishop Michael Nazir-Ali, who perceived that, in the Middle East, "the choice is not between angels and monsters but between one kind of monster and another. With all my experience, I cannot say that President Assad is the worst of all."

Caroline agreed with Nazir-Ali's assessment. "Assad is not the worst monster in the region," she said. "Attempts by the UK and others to forcibly remove him from power could create a political vacuum and provide a dangerous opportunity for ISIS-related Islamist extremists. Since there is presently no viable moderate armed opposition in Syria, enforced regime change would create a chaotic situation similar to – or perhaps even worse than – in Iraq or Libya." She would later reiterate this view in a co-authored letter to *The Times*.

She was also puzzled somewhat by what she called, "the gross double standards of Her Majesty's Government's policies." She said in 2018:

> *Saudi Arabia has far less than an unblemished record of human rights – yet earlier this year the Saudi Crown Prince received a royal welcome at Buckingham Palace and by the Prime Minister at Downing Street. Meanwhile the UK continues to promote trade with Sudan, whose president has been indicted by the International Criminal Court and whose government are responsible for the deaths of 3 million people, including their genocidal policies in Darfur, South Kordofan and Blue Nile – I have witnessed those myself – and the displacement of 5 million people, while still perpetrating gross violations of human rights in Sudan.*

Despite the pushback, Baroness Cox was committed to making her first journey to Syria in 2016 – to listen, to learn, and to stand in solidarity with all those who were suffering. Following receipt of her invitation, she dutifully notified the Foreign Office. In response she received an angry reprimand, and the demand to confer with then minister Tobias Ellwood.

"I was required to carry out a telephone call," she later explained. "The conversation began with a fierce opposition to my visit, instructing me that that it was 'too dangerous' and that the UK had no diplomatic representation, so there was no one to help if I got into trouble. I responded in the following way:

> *Minister, earlier this year I was in Sudan's Nuba Mountains when the military regime in Khartoum was bombing its own people with Antonovs. They fled to the mountains, hiding in caves with deadly snakes. I climbed a mountain to be with the people and met them in the caves; I also met a girl who had been bitten by a cobra but had survived. I was able to report on their horrendous predicament. This is how I use my role in the House of Lords, Minister.*

Caroline then describes that he proceeds to change tack – he told her:

> *I would "ruin British foreign policy". I made it clear that I was the "new kid on the block" and assured him that I knew very little about British foreign policy in Syria. I was then instructed to read the Foreign Office policy statement which referred to "regime change" on virtually every page.*

Throughout the conflict, the British government has persisted in declaring that the present regime has lost its legitimacy. They are committed to the mantra that "Assad must go" and continue to pursue a policy of attempting to remove the president from power, while maintaining a military presence in Syria to ensure "stabilisation".

Yet everyone Caroline met in Syria – including religious leaders, opposition parliamentarians, and local residents – described how they were terrified of the UK's support for "forced regime change". One local community leader in Maaloula went so far as to say that that he'd been an opponent of Assad and had joined the demonstrations against him. He would later declare, "Now I would die for him."

Beyond question, Caroline's decision to visit Syria and her meeting with President Assad stirred up controversy in Britain. But despite the naysayers, the small group packed their bags and embarked on their provocative and profoundly moving journey.

A visit and a letter to *The Times*

Early in their trip, the group made their way to Saidnaya, a historic Christian town located in the mountains north of Damascus. It had been attacked in 2012 by 2–3,000 militants armed with tanks and advanced weaponry. In response to the attack, some 300 local people had formed a popular defence militia. Thirty of them were killed. But after three days of intense conflict, that brave local force repelled the heavily armed jihadis. They saved Saidnaya from occupation.

Caroline and her colleagues spoke to Nabil, who had served as the leader of Saidnaya's local defence force. He explained, "My brother died in the fighting not far from here. My two cousins also died. I returned from Dubai to defend my village from al Nusra and Jaish al-Islam. They were supported by militants from Lebanon, France, Germany, Colombia and even some of my neighbours."

The Mother Superior of the nearby monastery of the Virgin Mary, described the victory in different terms: "When the terrorists came, we were not afraid. In the Bible it says that perfect love drives out fear. So we remained."

While Baroness Cox was visiting internally displaced people in Latakia, one of their administrators explained to her why he had to flee his home. "The Jihadists stopped all food supplies and placed snipers in the mountains who shot at us," he recounted. "We had no medical care for those who were wounded, and we had to use clothes as bandages... After the continuous siege we decided to escape from the village. As we ran, some went to the Turkish border, some to Idlib. A group of 130 who fled to Idlib were captured and killed." He went on to make a salient point: "The media say that the majority flee from the brutality of the Syrian government. But in Latakia we had safety. I don't need the kind of 'freedom' the jihadists are calling for."

Caroline recalls,

> So many of those we met there had been forced to
> flee the horrific suffering inflicted by the jihadists.
> The government provided them with as good
> accommodation as was possible – in their case a
> sports college. Although each family had to live in
> one room, at least they had water, electricity, toilets
> and cooking facilities. I will never forget meeting one
> of the many Muslim women who had been widowed.
> She had seen her husband and son killed before her

eyes, along with other relatives.

This grief-stricken woman told Baroness Cox, "War is terrible! You get killed by shelling from both sides. But on one side you die from bombings. On the other, you die from bombings and beheadings – and we don't want the beheadings!" The two women – from such very different worlds – simply hugged each other and wept together.

So it was, that despite the negativity surrounding Baroness Cox's decision to visit Syria, the trip was deeply rewarding thanks to her visits to cities, towns and villages where plain-spoken people eagerly shared their war stories. "Many were tragic," she later explained, "yet powerfully full of faith and immense courage."

Baroness Cox recalls,

> *When I returned to Britain, I sought to raise their concerns in the House of Lords. The Minister reprimanded me from the Dispatch Box. But I received a significant amount of support from Peers across the House. Shortly after the 'telling off' by the Minister, three former British Ambassadors (Peter Ford, Lord Green of Deddington, and Lord Wright of Richmond) and I wrote the following letter to* The Times, *dated 16 December 2016:*

> *Sir, Those of us who have served as ambassadors to Syria or who have visited Syria recently remain deeply concerned by Britain's continued support for the so-called moderate armed opposition and the British government's commitment to impose regime change. Civilians in many parts of Syria*

> *fear that such intervention will create a political*
> *vacuum, providing a dangerous opportunity for*
> *ISIS-related Islamist extremists. We therefore*
> *urge the prime minister and foreign secretary to*
> *respect the right of the Syrian people as a whole*
> *to choose their own future. Failing to do so not*
> *only undermines the long-term stability of Syria*
> *but risks creating a chaotic situation similar to, or*
> *perhaps even worse than, those in Iraq and Libya.*

As the former British First Sea Lord and Chief of Naval Staff, Lord West of Spithead, later concluded during a debate in the House of Lords:

> [The UK's] Syria strategy – if we actually have one –
> is prolonging the civil war, when ending the civil war
> is the best thing for the poor, benighted people of
> that country. Our focus seems to have been, from
> day one, regime change: presumably, not to hand
> over to the hotchpotch of opposition forces, many
> of which are worse than Daesh [ISIS]... Surely, our
> aim must now be to put a stop to the war as quickly
> as possible, accepting that the loathsome Assad is
> inevitably part of the equation.
>
> **Hansard, 15 May 2018, vol. 791, col. 583**

Baroness Cox has revisited Syria more than once following that initial 2016 trip, meeting local communities and internally displaced people in Damascus, Latakia, Saidnaya, Homs, Aleppo, and Maaloula. The day before her third journey there in April 2018, the US, UK, and France announced their intention to launch missile attacks in response to the alleged use of chemical weapons by the Syrian government in Douma. "We believe," she responded to a concerned questioner, "that it is especially important to visit Syria at this time to show solidarity with the Syrian people."

Coalition bombs and sanctions

According to Dapo Akande, Professor of Public International Law at the University of Oxford, the legal justification for the allied military action in April 2018 was "significantly flawed... not in accordance with the United Nations Charter and international law" and was dependent on a "radical restructuring of the most fundamental rules of the international legal order."

In fact, neither the United Nations nor the Organisation for the Prohibition of Chemical Weapons (OPCW) investigated the Douma attack before retaliatory missiles were fired. The US-led coalition did not have conclusive proof of the use of chemical weapons, or, if such an attack had occurred, by whom.

In the UK, then Prime Minister Theresa May did not seek parliamentary backing in advance of the bombing raids. Despite her defence of the "right to act quickly in the national interest", in Baroness Cox's view, the British government had exhibited a blatant disregard for the necessary checks and assessments on intelligence information.

In response to the bombings, three Orthodox patriarchs in Syria issued a statement,

> This brutal aggression is a clear violation of
> international laws and the UN Charter, because
> it is an unjustified assault on a sovereign country,

> a member of the UN. It causes us great pain that
> this assault comes from powerful countries to
> which Syria did not cause any harm in any way...
> This brutal aggression destroys the chances for a
> peaceful political solution and leads to escalation
> and more complications.

By 2020, as the conflict entered its tenth year, escalating numbers of local Syrians expressed to Caroline dismay and anger at the devastating impact of British foreign policy – not only because of its continuing support for "forced regime change" but because of the imposition of a complex network of economic sanctions.

"I am told that the aim of these sanctions," Caroline explained, "is to compel the Syrian regime to change its behaviour. But they have not removed President Assad. Nor have they resulted in any meaningful political concessions by his administration. Contrary to their stated intentions, sanctions have contributed to a worsening of the humanitarian crisis in Syria."

In August 2020, as the Covid-19 pandemic raged around the world, a group of UN experts raised the same concerns. They warned that "Sanctions that were imposed in the name of delivering human rights are in fact killing people and depriving them of fundamental rights, including the rights to health, to food and to life itself." They called for the sanctions to "be lifted – or at a minimum eased – so people can get basics like soap and disinfectants to stay healthy, and so that hospitals can get ventilators and other equipment to keep people alive."

Caroline followed up the UN experts' warning with a letter in January 2021 to Prime Minister Boris Johnson – which was co-signed by over eighty international diplomats, academics, and some of the most senior church leaders in the Middle East – urging him "to help Syrians to alleviate a humanitarian crisis".

Her heartfelt belief is that economic sanctions are among the biggest causes of suffering for the Syrian people. Yet sanctions have only increased in recent years, even as conflict continues, and at a time when thousands of Syrians are dying of Covid-19.

The shattered village of Maaloula

In June 2019 Italian writer Daniele Rocchi beautifully described Maaloula – a unique and picturesque historic village which is dear to the heart of Baroness Cox. In his article for SIR news agency Rocchi wrote,

> Maaloula is a Christian stronghold in Syria where Aramaic, the language of Jesus Christ, is still spoken today... Before the war Maaloula was a pilgrimage destination for many pilgrims arriving from all over the world. Every year they would travel to these mountains to pray in one of the birthplaces of Syrian Christianity. Today Maaloula is a village that still bears the scars of the war, with deep wounds inflicted on the local community, disfiguring its churches, its icons, its paintings, its statues. This was where a nine-month battle was fought, from September 2013 to May 2014.
>
> **taken from 'Syria: the challenge faced by the Christian population of Maaloula where there's no more time to look back'**

While several global powers continued their *danse macabre*

around the use of weapons of mass destruction, Syria's ancient Christian village of Maaloula was attacked by rebel forces – some of them affiliated with al-Qaeda.

On 11 September 2013, a source inside Syria reported,

> More than 30 Christians are missing, six have
> been killed, we have the names of three of them.
> The Mor Serkis monastery has been bombed,
> but we don't know about the damage. Most of
> the residents fled to Damascus; those who have
> not been able to get out of their houses because
> of ongoing fights between opposition groups and
> Syrian military have remained in Maaloula. The
> Jabhat al Nusra, Free Syrian Army and the Syrian
> army have occupied Maaloula.

Unlike countless other cases, which are barely noted in the Western media, Maaloula received attention because the scenic town – a popular tourist site – is on a list of candidates for UNESCO World Heritage site designation.

The violence there was tragically reflected in an AFP report in which Rasha, a young Maaloula woman, described a phone conversation that took place when she was trying to locate her fiancé, Atef.

"I rang his mobile phone and one of them answered," she said.

"Good morning, Rashrush," a voice answered, using her nickname. "We are from the Free Syrian Army. Do you know your fiancé was a member of the *Shabiha* [pro-government militia] who was carrying weapons? We have slit his throat."

The man told her Atef had been given the option of converting to Islam, but had refused.

"Jesus didn't come to save him," he mockingly informed her.

In 2016 Baroness Cox travelled from Damascus to Maaloula. "We had the poignant privilege of standing in a room where three men (one as young twenty-two) had been martyred for refusing to convert from Christianity to Islam... meanwhile every holy place in the village was utterly desecrated."

Caroline met with a group of widows who had returned to the city after the battle and were trying to rebuild their homes and their lives. They were industriously collecting wild fruits and vegetables, which they pickled and sold. This helped to alleviate the food shortage and enabled them to make some money.

Inspired by what she saw and heard, Baroness Cox's visit to Maaloula provided her with the opportunity to establish a partnership between HART and the Syrian St Ephrem Patriarchal Development Committee (EPDC). This initiated a programme to help women develop entrepreneurial projects. "It's our hope that those women," Caroline explains, "who have lost everything, will find means to rebuild their lives and to support their families."

Touching the wounds

Baroness Cox also visited Aleppo, even when its eastern sector was still in the hands of jihadists. One particular visit by the group was arranged by an Armenian evangelical pastor, Harout Silimian. On the evening the group arrived, the community celebrated their presence with an outdoor banquet. The guest list included imams, muftis and Yazidis, as well as clergy from several Christian denominations.

"Bombs fell around us continuously," Caroline recalls. "We were only 350 meters from the jihadist frontline. But throughout the meal, a quintet played beautiful music. That's the spirit of the Armenians: music continues even while the bombs fall!"

The following morning, Baroness Cox joined the others in a service at one of the Armenian churches. Also in attendance were Muslim clerics, Christian church leaders, and the Yazidi representatives. A children's choir sang beautifully, even as bombs continued to fall.

A Roman Catholic bishop told the congregation:

> In Aleppo, we had months without water. The
> terrorists tried to destroy our history of 2,000
> years, with the theft of archaeological sites. They
> destroyed what they couldn't steal. We hope
> you can help us to rebuild our heritage. Syria is
> a mosaic of different people. In West Aleppo,
> faith leaders, Muslim and Christian, are under
> threat. Before the kidnapping of the bishops,
> four Muslim leaders were killed. Western media
> does not tell correctly what is happening in Syria.
> We have human rights and humanity, so we ask
> you to report the reality of our suffering and the
> injustice.

Caroline Cox relates what came next.

> *After the service, a Chaldean Catholic priest spoke to
> me, and I will never forget his words. He recounted
> the story of "Doubting Thomas" – the disciple who
> was not present when Christ appeared to the others
> after His resurrection. When they told him of Jesus'
> appearance, Thomas said, "I'm not going to believe
> unless He comes to me and I put my hands in his
> wounded hands and side." Then, suddenly Jesus*

appeared to him and invited him to put his hands into His wounds. He told Thomas, "Now that you have seen you can believe. So go and tell!"

Then that priest offered one of the most simple and powerful messages I have ever received:

"Thank you for coming to visit us. Like Thomas, you came to put your hands into the wounds of our suffering. Now that you have seen, you can believe. Go and tell!"

Caroline explains, "His words sum up what HART's mission is all about. We cannot feel the anguish others have suffered. But we can put our hands into the wounds of their suffering. Then we can believe, go, and tell."

Chapter Eight

Conclusion – On the Home Front

The sun has barely risen, and Caroline Cox is parked along an empty, narrow side street in London, with the engine still running. She keeps checking the car's rear-view mirrors to make sure that no one has followed her.

It is 7 a.m. Any minute now, a young woman in her early twenties – who we'll call Liyana – will walk into the side street, stand at a designated red post box, and place her handbag on the pavement.

"It was one of the most surreal and poignant moments of my life", Baroness Cox later recalled. "We had arranged to meet at this secret location. But there was no guarantee that Liyana was safe. Clearly, we needed to drive away quickly!"

Caroline flashes the car headlights, pulls up to the post box and greets Liyana with her characteristic reassuring smile. It is their first meeting, but Liyana responds with a deep sigh of relief and settles into the car. She has been waiting for this moment for a long time. As the door closes and the car begins to accelerate, she clutches her handbag tightly – she's carrying minimal possessions so not to arouse suspicion. And undetected, they drive away from London to a safe house far away.

Liyana was escaping her family home. For years, she had been living in an unhappy and controlling environment, required to work in her father's news agency, and prevented from using her degree or pursuing her own career. Even worse, she also faced the prospect of being sent to Pakistan against her will, and possibly forced into an arranged marriage.

"As she began to tell her story," Caroline Cox said, "it dawned on me that this wonderful and courageous young woman was leaving everything she knew behind. She was driving towards freedom. But she was saying goodbye, possibly forever, to her family, her home and her closest friends. It was an emotionally ambivalent journey – a mixture of celebration and apprehension." Liyana has since enjoyed her freedom and sends grateful, happy messages to Caroline. They have also enjoyed tea together in the House of Lords!

Sadly, however, Liyana's story exposes the mere tip of the iceberg. Countless other women and girls in the UK suffer repeated and severe forms of abuse within their homes. Many such victims have reached out to Caroline. They report feeling pressured and disowned: they are sworn at, beaten, burned, psychologically manipulated, sexually abused, and treated like slaves. Among some of these women, their suffering is worsened by the nature of the closed communities in which they live, where great pressure exists not to seek "outside" professional help – a choice that might be deemed to bring shame or dishonour on the family.

During recent periods of Covid-19 lockdowns, UK government restrictions have required residents to "Stay safe" and "Stay home". Yet, for victims of domestic abuse, honour-based abuse, or forced marriage, home is the least safe place to be. As a 2020 Women's Aid Survivor Survey reports,

> The pandemic has escalated abuse and closed
> down routes to safety for victims to escape...
> Women in lockdown with their abuser will be less
> able to get breathing space. It will be harder to
> text or phone to get support from friends and
> family, and from specialist support services. Child
> survivors will no longer have the respite of school
> or nursery, which can often be a safe space to
> access support.

During Covid-19, household isolation has created new tensions, worsened abusive situations, and increased anxiety for those who feel at risk.

Equal and Free

"We cannot sit here complacently on our red and green benches while women are suffering in ways which would make our Suffragettes turn in their graves," said Baroness Cox to her colleagues in Parliament in 2011, as she embarked on a new campaign to alleviate the suffering of these women and girls. "If we don't do something," she went on to say, "we are condoning it."

In step with this mandate, she launched a new organisation – Equal and Free – to work alongside those affected by abuse, with the help of lawyers, academics, and women's groups. Together, this coalition of survivors and activists began to speak up, publishing reports, hosting events, and writing articles. Using her role in the House of Lords, Baroness Cox instigated dozens of parliamentary debates to raise awareness and to hasten the introduction of meaningful legislation.

Read the official record of these debates, and you'll soon lose count of how many people speak of Caroline's expertise and compassion, summed up by government spokesperson Lord Keen of Elie: "I join all sides of the House in putting on the record my admiration not only for the determination of the noble Baroness, Lady Cox, but for the courage of the women to whom she has listened" (Hansard, 27 January, 2017, vol. 778, col. 918).

In a 2015 blog, Sir Gerald Howarth, former MP for Aldershot, described her as the "go-to expert" on these issues:

> She is respected by parliamentarians of all parties and, more importantly, trusted by women's groups who support victims of abuse. For years, she has been raising these issues in parliament, instigating debates, representing the oppressed, and holding our Government to account.

During one such debate, Baroness Cox referred to the case of Caitlin Spencer (not her real name), a victim of sex grooming in the UK, who from the age of fourteen was controlled, repeatedly raped, forced to drink alcohol, given drugs, sold, and passed on to new gangs over and over again. Her abusers were blatant in their attacks on her, often picking her up her from school or home, taking her to flats they owned, family homes, or hotels booked for the day, only to be horrifically and systematically abused.

Caitlin recorded her story in *The Sunday Times'* top ten bestseller *Please, Let Me Go: The Horrific True Story of a Girl's Life in the Hands of Sex Traffickers* (London: John Blake, 2017). She writes,

> To Baroness Caroline Cox – you and Sam
> [a colleague of Baroness Cox] have been so
> supportive and helpful through so many things
> and I would always want you to be on my team.
> You have helped get my voice heard in so many
> ways. I'm blessed to have you as a friend.

Caitlin did not receive the help that she needed following her horrendous trauma. She had to fund her own psychotherapy, with help from friends. She still sees her abusers driving their taxis with impunity – just as many other victims still see perpetrators living freely and continuing to intimidate them.

According to Baroness Cox, one of the greatest obstacles to justice is that people in positions of authority sometimes dismiss the evidence of victims, or minimise it, and fail to call the perpetrators to account. As she said during a Grand Committee debate in May 2019,

> [Many victims] report feeling let down by the
> police and social services. They have often
> been met with a lack of understanding and
> feel that their stories are not believed. Some
> are told that they "brought it on themselves"
> or that they "must have consented" to being
> raped... The success of prosecutions depends
> on witnesses and survivors coming forward
> and testifying. Young girls who have already
> suffered so much must not be deterred from
> reaching out for help... The scale of suffering
> far exceeds the preventive measures and
> support for victims that are currently in place.
> Until comprehensive action is taken, politicians'

promises of "never again" will continue to
remain unfulfilled.

Hansard, 14 May 2019, vol. 797, col. 78GC

In another horrific case, a consultant gynaecologist described
to Baroness Cox a request from a 63-year-old man to repair the
hymen of his 23-year-old wife. The gynaecologist refused as this
is an illegal operation in the UK, whereupon the man became
intensely angry. He claimed that doctors in his town, not far from
London, frequently undertake this operation under another
name. He wanted this surgical procedure for his wife in order to
take her back to their country of origin to marry another man.
Her next husband could then obtain a visa to enter the UK.
He would probably abuse and then divorce his wife and marry
another, or take more wives here. The man who asked for this
operation said that he earned about £10,000 for effecting this
arrangement. He explained that this was very helpful, as he was
unemployed.

"Marriages" that are not marriages

Although people from any faith tradition (or none) may suffer
abuse, Baroness Cox works particularly closely with Muslim
women who have endured severe religiously sanctioned gender
discrimination. They face extra barriers from within their own
communities because of the application of established Shari'a
law principles, which inherently discriminate against women
and girls.

Theresa May, before she became prime minister, was the
first government minister to acknowledge the severity of this

problem when she said in speech to the Foundation for Peace in 2015,

> There are some areas where – like in the
> application of Shari'a law – we know enough to
> know we have a problem, but we do not yet know
> the full extent of the problem... There is evidence
> of women being "divorced" under Shari'a law and
> left in penury, wives who are forced to return to
> abusive relationships because Shari'a councils say
> a husband has a right to "chastise", and Shari'a
> councils giving the testimony of a woman only
> half the weight of the testimony of a man.

The then Home Secretary commissioned an independent review to examine these concerns and to explore whether Shari'a law was being misused or applied in a way that was incompatible with domestic law. Were there discriminatory practices against women who are under the authority of Shari'a councils?

The review's findings were alarming. It revealed that women who are married in Islamic ceremonies – but who are not married under English law – can suffer grave disadvantages because they lack legal protection. They often only discover their lack of official marital status when their relationship breaks down. They have no legal rights against their "husband" and have no option of obtaining a civil divorce.

The same concerns were highlighted in a Channel 4 survey in 2017, which found that six in ten Muslim women who have had traditional Islamic weddings in Britain are not legally married. Of these, over a quarter (twenty-eight per cent) are not aware that they do not have the same rights as they would have with a legally recognised marriage.

A further study by the Muslim women's group Aurat: Supporting Women highlighted cases of women in Britain living in polygamous marriages. The evidence for its findings published in 2014 was drawn from fifty case studies of Muslim women living in the West Midlands. Two thirds of those who identified as being married said their husband had more than one wife. The findings of these reports are all the more alarming when it is estimated that as many as 100,000 couples in Britain are living in Islamic marriages not recognised by English law.

Over the years, many such women have reached out to Baroness Cox. They have come to her desperate, destitute, and even suicidal, trapped in unhappy polygamous marriages, or with no rights following asymmetrical divorces instigated by their husbands. One lady, called Roma, was physically abused by her husband, an overseas student. She was in such fear of being rejected by her community that she did everything possible to avoid a divorce. When her husband could not obtain a visa, he sent Roma an Islamic divorce by post. She told Baroness Cox,

> [My husband] sent me an Islamic divorce; written briefly on a plain piece of paper was "I divorce you" three times. My world was toppled. It's difficult to explain how it feels. I never received a kiss, hug or any form of appreciation. The Imams told me to have patience – "you will be rewarded on the day of judgment." Unfortunately, Shari'a law accepts this three-word form of divorce, where no consent from me is needed, and my opinion is not sought. I felt that plain piece of paper was a mockery of my human rights.

Another lady, called Padda, told Baroness Cox that she started having marriage problems in 2014:

> My husband during one argument said to me: "I divorce you." He left me and the kids for another woman. We had contact over the kids for a while but in 2016 I received a divorce certificate through the post. The certificate explained that I was divorced. I was not notified by the Shari'a council that my husband had asked for a divorce. I was not even approached by them to ask me if I agreed. There was no mediation between us to sort this out. I called the number that sent me the divorce certificate, but the number was incorrect. I called the main Shari'a council to ask them to explain if they had a local office, but the man was very rude and put the phone down on me. I feel that I didn't even get a say in the so-called divorce and was left with two small children to take care of by myself. I personally think that I am not divorced as it was done completely unacceptably, and I was not contacted at any point during the process to see how I felt about anything. As a woman I felt so alone, as if I was left by myself to face a divorce I never wanted and to deal with my emotions while looking after two kids. I think the council of this so-called Islamic law is very wrong in the way they deal with the woman's side and did not give me a chance to even hear my side. It basically hears what a man wants and that's it.

And then there was Aala (a pseudonym), who was originally from Pakistan and also had an Islamic marriage in the UK. She was raped, abused, and financially exploited by her husband. Her imam and her husband refused to negotiate an Islamic divorce, claiming that the marriage had never taken place, despite the fact that she had a video recording of the ceremony. She told Caroline, weeping, that she is now so ostracised by her community, both in the UK and in Pakistan, and that she feels such shame and loneliness that she has attempted suicide.

The cases of Roma, Padda, and Aala are not unique. Thousands of other Muslim women have suffered in similar ways. "This cannot be allowed to continue," wrote Caroline in a 2015 report entitled "A Parallel World". "Provisions must be introduced to ensure that the operation of Shari'a law principles in the UK today is not undermining the rights of women and the rule of law."

Attempts to change the law

Since launching Equal and Free almost ten years ago, Baroness Cox has submitted eight bills before Parliament, all of which seek to enshrine the rights of Muslim women who do not yet have the protection of legal marriage. She has also tabled amendments to other bills, submitted proposals for Special Committees, provided evidence to inquiries, written numerous papers, and given tens of media interviews. All such initiatives have received cross-party support – including from senior parliamentarians Lord Carlile of Berriew QC, Lord Dholakia, and Lord Singh of Wimbledon – as well as support from organisations concerned with the suffering of these vulnerable women, such as the inspirational Muslim Women's Advisory Council, Karma

Nirvana, BASIRA (British Arabs Supporting Universal Women's Rights), and the internationally renowned Canadian Muslim scholar Raheel Raza.

"When I first raised these concerns in Parliament, I was lambasted for meddling in private religious matters," Baroness Cox reflected recently:

> *Some even called me "anti-Muslim" and*
> *"Islamophobic" – a rather perplexing rationale, given*
> *that my bills were drafted on the basis of advice*
> *from Muslim women and that their very purpose*
> *is to ensure greater protections for Muslim women.*
> *Granted, this is a sensitive and complex topic, with*
> *no simple answers – I have never pretended to know*
> *all of the answers – but that is no reason to ignore it!*

As Jerome Taylor said, writing for *The Independent* in 2011, following the introduction of her first bill: "If there is one thing Baroness Caroline Cox is not afraid of it is whipping up controversy." And, in fact, after a decade of campaigns, Baroness Cox's concerns no longer seem obscure nor controversial. There is now mainstream recognition of the suffering endured by Muslim women who do not have the protection of legal marriage.

- In December 2016, the Casey Review, commissioned by the government, agreed with Baroness Cox that "all marriages, regardless of faith, should be registered so that the union is legally valid under British laws. We have heard strong arguments that the Marriage Act should be reformed to apply to all faiths and that faith institutions must ensure they are properly registered and operate within existing legislation."

- In February 2018, the Independent Review into the Application of Shari'a Law, commissioned by the government, similarly concluded: "By linking Islamic marriage to civil marriage it ensures that a greater number of women will have the full protection afforded to them in family law and the right to a civil divorce, lessening the need to attend and simplifying the decision process of [Shari'a] councils."

- In March 2018, the government published its Integrated Communities Strategy Green Paper, stating: "The Government is supportive in principle of the requirement that civil marriages are conducted before or at the same time as religious ceremonies. Therefore, the Government will explore the legal and practical challenges of limited reform relating to the law on marriage and religious weddings."

- In January 2019, the Parliamentary Assembly of the Council of Europe passed a resolution, which echoed Caroline's concerns and urged the UK to "review the Marriage Act to make it a legal requirement for Muslim couples to civilly register their marriage before or at the same time as their Islamic ceremony."

- In September 2020, the Law Commission launched a public consultation on proposals "to modernise and improve wedding law" to address problems associated with religious-only weddings.

"We will have to wait and see what comes next," Baroness Cox says. "There is much to be encouraged by – thanks to the heroic efforts of the courageous Muslim women and the many groups who support them. Together, we have made important progress. But we must remain active and vigilant."

She continues,

> *I have seen little evidence in ten years to suggest that promises by the government to "continue the exploration of reform" will not be used to postpone viable legislation or to kick our serious concerns into the long grass. The government's response to date (or lack thereof) is, at best, demonstrative of their failure to keep pace with social changes and cultural-religious practices. At worst, it exposes an unwillingness to protect one of this country's most marginalised, excluded, and discriminated-against groups. Such shocking cases of gender discrimination cannot be allowed to continue. The rights of Muslim women must be upheld.*

Eyewitness to a broken world

Indeed, Baroness Cox's determination to uphold women's rights in her home country mirrors her dedication to human rights and religious freedom across the globe. As we've seen, in the midst of some of the most dangerous and unjustly governed nations, as well as in far-flung locations where the intrusion of bloodshed threatens the lives of innocents, Baroness Cox has long persevered in her efforts.

She possesses a rare and unique combination of gifts. On the one hand she demonstrates willingness to practise hands-on care for those who are in need and in pain. She began her professional career as trained nurse, and her natural instinct to physically embrace the suffering, to literally wipe away tears, and to provide one-to-one comfort to the starving, sick and dying has never diminished.

However, at the same time, her appointment as a life peer in the House of Lords has added another key element to the caregiving dimension of Caroline's nature: the ability to speak to her government and others in authority about the realities on the ground in some of the world's worst trouble spots. As we've seen, she has persistently reported her experiences in her official capacity, as well as including in her accounts the best practical and political suggestions she can provide, in the hope of bringing help and healing to those who need it most.

Finally, but above all, Baroness Cox's Christian faith has given her a sense of mission and personal ministry. Caroline recognises – along with those who know and love her – that her work amid some the world's most persistent conflicts and unstaunched wounds is a sacred calling, a spiritual obligation, and a priceless opportunity to be a "voice for the voiceless". And for all of us who stand and watch and pray, Baroness Cox duly serves as our trustworthy eyewitness to a broken world.

Index

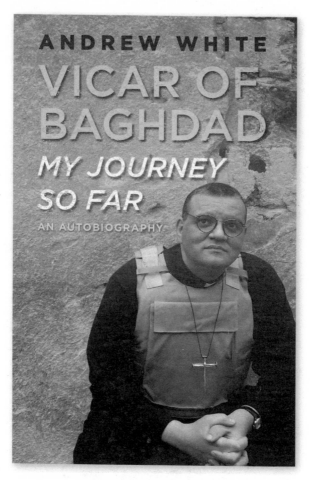

ISBN: 978 0 7459 8119 2

e-ISBN: 978 0 7459 8145 1

'This story will infuse faith, hope and love.'
Revd Canon J. John

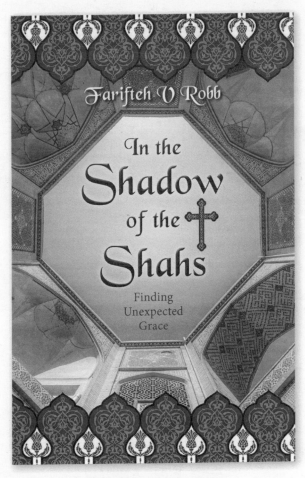

Fariftch V Robb

In the
Shadow
of the ✝
Shahs

Finding
Unexpected
Grace

ISBN: 978 0 7459 8088 1

e-ISBN: 978 0 7459 8089 8

'A beautifully written autobiography of a remarkable life'

John Clark, Friends of the Diocese of Iran